Living with Theory

Blackwell Manifestos

In this new series major critics make timely interventions to address important concepts and subjects, including topics as diverse as, for example: Culture, Race, Religion, History, Society, Geography, Literature, Literary Theory, Shakespeare, Cinema, and Modernism. Written accessibly and with verve and spirit, these books follow no uniform prescription but set out to engage and challenge the broadest range of readers, from undergraduates to postgraduates, university teachers and general readers – all those, in short, interested in on-going debates and controversies in the humanities and social sciences.

Already Published

Living with Theory

Vincent B. Leitch

Blackwell Publishing

BLACKWELL PUBLISHING

350 Main Street, Malden, MA 02148-5020, USA
9600 Garsington Road, Oxford OX4 2DQ, UK
550 Swanston Street, Carlton, Victoria 3053, Australia

The right of Vincent B. Leitch to be identified as the author of this work has been asserted in accordance with the UK Copyright, Designs, and Patents Act 1988.

Designations used by companies to distinguish their products are often claimed as trademarks. All brand names and product names used in this book are trade names, service marks, trademarks, or registered trademarks of their respective owners. The publisher is not associated with any product or vendor mentioned in this book.

This publication is designed to provide accurate and authoritative information in regard to the subject matter covered. It is sold on the understanding that the publisher is not engaged in rendering professional services. If professional advice or other expert assistance is required, the services of a competent professional should be sought.

First published 2008 by Blackwell Publishing Ltd

1 2008

Library of Congress Cataloging-in-Publication Data

Leitch, Vincent B., 1944–
    Living with theory / Vincent B. Leitch.
        p. cm.— (Blackwell manifestos)
    Includes bibliographical references and index.
    ISBN 978-1-4051-7529-6 (hardcover : alk. paper)—ISBN 978-1-4051-7528-9 (pbk. : alk. paper)
1. Criticism—History—20th century. 2. Literature, Modern—History and criticism—Theory, etc.
I. Title.
PN94.L393 2008
801′.95—dc22

                                        2007015881

A catalogue record for this title is available from the British Library.

Set in 11.5/13.5pt Bembo
by SPi Publisher Services, Pondicherry, India.
Printed and bound in Singapore
by Markono Print Media Pte Ltd

The publisher's policy is to use permanent paper from mills that operate a sustainable forestry policy, and which has been manufactured from pulp processed using acid-free and elementary chlorine-free practices. Furthermore, the publisher ensures that the text paper and cover board used have met acceptable environmental accreditation standards.

For further information on
Blackwell Publishing, visit our website at
www.blackwellpublishing.com

Contents

Preface

The message of *Living with Theory* is that theory is not what it used to be. It has an expansive thriving present and a promising future. A renaissance of literary and cultural theory began in the 1970s and continues today. Faculty and students in North American and British institutions of higher education and elsewhere nowadays have a much wider range of materials to examine and a vastly expanded toolkit of methods, devices, and perspectives to employ. I for one do not long for or personally miss the previous era's insulating aestheticism, obsessive stylistic analysis, predictable search for image patterns and archetypes, and thin history. Mainstream academic literary criticism particularly in the US was then an inward-looking, spiritualized, ascetic enterprise. It warned against the heresy of paraphrase, fearing the connection of literature to life. It advocated impersonal pseudo-scientific analysis and rooted out methodological fallacies. It fetishized texts as, of all things, spatial objects. This whole late modern cultural operation felt very much like a turn away from the world and a replacement for dogmatic religion. In contrast, contemporary postmodern theory has been and remains expansive and worldly, responsive to society and culture, engaged with social history and political economy, and dedicated to discovery and invention rather than purification of method and curating high culture. Like its predecessor, it continuously sifts and reinvigorates traditions of theory and literature from ancient times to the present, although its historical preoccupations are different. Most noteworthy, contemporary theory has a special penchant for exploring

1

margins, contradictions, countercurrents, and resistances, unlike the earlier period's obsession with unity, harmony, balance, and wholeness.

One of the features most characteristic of today's postindustrial consumer societies is the proliferation and disaggregation of separate spheres and niches. As a consequence, the big picture often seems unknowable. This brings about bewilderment and spawns much-needed guides and cognitive maps. Whether today's postmodern consumer is buying a breakfast cereal, a movie DVD, a retirement mutual fund, or a new vehicle, there are so many kinds and choices that trustworthy guides, top 30 lists, rating services, and recognizable brand names seem essential to cut through the baffling, but structurally typical, disarray. *Living with Theory* maps the highly disorganized field of contemporary theory in the context of today's literary and cultural studies. Yet going beyond the cliché of cultural disorganization, it factors into its account how things hang together. It considers ongoing postmodernization and globalization, multiculturalism and culture wars, free-market economics and the attenuation of the welfare state, plus the recent rise of the corporate university. Essential for understanding today's criticism and theory, such economic, political, and social phenomena would have been ruled out of consideration by the dominant theory of the preceding era.

Addressing outsiders and insiders, *Living with Theory* begins with six contending definitions of theory. Part I expounds and defends theory's infrastructure, its teaching, its extensions of critical reading, and its fusions with other disciplines. Along the way it sketches possible futures. Part II offers contrasting case studies of the political turn of theory that since the 1990s has become ever more critical of late capitalism's increasingly triumphant free-market political economy. The chapters explore the vexing roles played in our time, first, by the key concept of sovereignty (grasped through Derridean deconstruction); and second, by the cruel restructuring of the academic labor force. Part III synthesizes wide-ranging representative recent changes, dramatic transformations and disorganizations in concepts of literature. It takes into account present-day political reconfigurations as well as recent textbooks, canons, and new modes of postnational literary

2

theory, history, and scholarship. Literature is not what it used to be a few short decades ago.

One of the main tasks, I believe, of criticism and theory, both literary and cultural, is engaged assessment, requiring evaluation of strengths and weaknesses. This job of work pertains whether scrutinizing texts, objects, performances, movements, figures, groups, or other phenomena. Neither admiration nor condemnation alone is enough. I learned this the hard way from the disinterested but often sycophantic formalist criticism in which I was raised for a decade during the 1960s and 1970s. So I advocate combining wide-ranging cultural critique and tightly focused technical analyses (so-called close readings). The details of such critical practices are outlined and employed across *Living with Theory*. Bad theorizing and use of theory should not escape such double-edged scrutiny.

What's wrong with contemporary theory? To listen to its opponents and critics, a great deal is amiss. It turns its attention away from literature and art in favor of popular culture and politics. It is obscure and difficult. It is both ubiquitous and mandatory in higher education, leaving no respectable space for doubters, who feel themselves victims. Perhaps most noteworthy, it is PC. Such charges emanate from all along the political spectrum. The epithet "politically correct" encapsulates a passel of related charges. Contemporary theory is preoccupied with matters of race, class, gender, and national identity. This preoccupation leads it to a focus on minorities and subalterns, obsessing about resistant and counterhegemonic social forces. It often risks being moralistic and antinationalistic. It ends up celebrating minor literatures and forms, including Third World and popular culture at the expense of the canon of great works of Western culture. Its fixation upon identity politics and multiculturalism entails an end to objectivity and humanism. It falls into cultural relativism. It casts each person as occupying a particular subject-position and standpoint, defined by race, class, gender, and national belonging (for instance, white working-class heterosexual American male versus human being). The result is that achieving social integration and national unity appears almost impossible.

3

Living with Theory responds to these charges across its eight chapters. It is a defense and a manifesto. But keep in mind a great deal of contention goes on within and among the many different camps of contemporary theory. Given the disorganization of the field, the word "theory" functions nowadays frequently as a banner of convenience as well as a symbolic marker of professional identity and also a bogeyman. It should come as no surprise, moreover, that contemporary theory answers to the post–Cold War corporate university of excellence, just as it did to the earlier postwar research university. It does so through its publicly acknowledged dedications: to productivity and growth, to new methods and interdisciplinarity, to publication and publicity, to modernization and diversity, and to the wide distribution of cultural capital. All that is to say, theory in academe forwards large social, political, and economic agendas.

Contemporary theory has made many significant contributions to scholarship and criticism. New concepts, methods, and traditions have been discovered by feminism, postcolonial and ethnic criticism, poststructuralism, psychoanalysis, Marxism, and many subfields of cultural studies such as body studies, subculture studies, and whiteness studies. Major figures have changed the way we look at the world. I am thinking, for example, of Harold Bloom, Judith Butler, Donna Haraway, Edward Said, plus the many French thinkers such as Louis Althusser, Pierre Bourdieu, Jacques Derrida, and Michel Foucault. There are contemporary theory classics that have dramatically altered our understanding like *The Anxiety of Influence, Of Grammatology, Discipline and Punish, Orientalism, The Madwoman in the Attic, Distinction, "A Manifesto for Cyborgs," Postmodernism, or the Cultural Logic of Late Capitalism, Gender Trouble.* In addition, there are dozens of invaluable innovative concepts stemming from contemporary theory. I have in mind, for instance, anxiety of influence, compulsory heterosexuality, cultural capital, cyborg, docile body, the male gaze, heteroglossia, hybridity, ideological state apparatus, interpretive communities, intertextuality, orientalism, rhizome, simulacra, whiteness. Two examples. The fact that an American like me is "white," being of Italian-Irish descent, is a recent phenomenon. A century ago my

4

ancestors were cast as nonwhite. When I walk into a classroom, I often take my unmarked color for granted, unlike my black colleagues. The social construction of race, white race included, plays a key role in identity formation. With the idea of heteroglossia, I conceive language not as impersonal signifiers, tropes, or grammatical rules, but as utterances from embodied subjects engaged in dialogue. Moreover, heteroglot discourse is stratified and centrifugal, composed of contending dialects, genres, and group languages (age, professional, and class groups). In this theory language is connected to the body, social class, multiple subject positions, ideology. It is not abstract or purely aesthetic. Heteroglossia applies to literary language. As mechanisms of discovery and speculative instruments, such concepts hold as bright a future as their recent past. More is to come from theory now increasingly part of the genetic code of contemporary humanities and social sciences across the globe. Nowadays theory is not a luxury.

Part I
Theory

1

Theory Ends

The theory renaissance of the late twentieth and early twenty-first century especially in North America has been marked by an unprecedented proliferation of schools and movements. In the US, for example, they range from the maturing of formalism, myth criticism, and the social criticism of the New York intellectuals to new developments in Marxism, psychoanalysis, and hermeneutics to the rise and spread of reader-response criticism, structuralism and semiotics, poststructuralism, feminism, and critical race theory to the emergence of postcolonial theory, new historicism, cultural studies, queer theory, and personal criticism. At the turn of the twenty-first century many branches of the newer movements and schools suddenly gathered together, more or less willingly, under the capacious banner of cultural studies, displacing the previously dominant banner of poststructuralism. These branches take the form nowadays of an increasingly disaggregated front characterized by several dozen recognized subfields: body studies, disability studies, whiteness studies, media studies, indigenous studies, narrative studies, porn studies, performance studies, working-class studies, popular culture studies, trauma studies, and so on.

As a consequence, theory in the current framework has at least a half dozen different meanings, each of which has a distinct reception history and set of effects. First, it refers loosely to the gamut of contemporary schools and movements, plus their offshoots in cultural studies. That is to say, it names the broad field and is synonymous with criticism. Starting in the 1980s and persisting to the present, conservative scholars dedicated to mid-century moral and formalist analysis of canonical literary works have waged a campaign against such theory.[1] Second, theory designates general principles and procedures — methods — as well as the self-reflection employed in all areas of literary and cultural studies. A small but vigorous skirmish against such theory has been enjoined by neopragmatists, who oppose foundational principles, with the result that few nowadays defend theory in its most ambitious methodological or scientific pretensions.[2] Third, theory is widely considered a toolbox of flexible, useful, and contingent devices and concepts, judged for their productivity and innovation. The critique of such pragmatic theory, small in scale, has come from various defenders of objective interpretation, ranging from curmudgeons committed to the old days before theory to defenders of formalism to much more challenging hermeneuticists.[3] Fourth, theory denotes professional common sense — what goes without saying and what every specialist knows — so that everyone in the field has a theory, although some people don't realize it. In this view theory is a sociohistorical construction complete with contradictions and blind spots yet shored up by the current status quo. But such equating of theory with professionally configured common sense paradoxically ends up diluting its specificity, its conflicts, and its socially critical agendas. Fifth, theory signifies more narrowly structuralism and poststructuralism, the works of Lévi-Strauss, Lacan, Foucault, Derrida, Deleuze, Kristeva, and company, plus their followers and imitators. This is frequently called high or grand theory, with low (or vernacular) theory and posttheory arriving after structuralism and poststructuralism.[4] Opposition has come to such briefly triumphant theory from not only conservative scholars, but also a broad array of contending liberal and left theorists, indicting it (particularly deconstruction) for philosophical idealism, nominalism, obscurantism, and quietism, charges early made famous by certain Marxists, feminists, critical race theorists, and cultural studies scholars.[5] The latter-day persistence of poststructuralism has appeared in two forms: its continued widespread use past its two-decade-long hegemony; its belated turn to ethics and politics. The latter occurred after the revelations in 1987 of Paul de Man's World War Two anti-Semitic writings, the symbolic moment that, nevertheless, marks the waning of poststructuralism as dominant theory and the broad spread of talk about new historicism, cultural studies, and posttheory. Sixth, theory names a historically new, postmodern mode of discourse that breaches longstanding borders, fusing literary criticism, philosophy, history, sociology, psychoanalysis, and politics.[6] This cross-disciplinary pastiche is, not surprisingly, subject to the broad critique of postmodernism, especially for its undermining the hard-won autonomy gained during modern times for both the university and the academic disciplines.

Starting in the early 1990s, we have regularly heard announcements of the end, death, or day after theory. But to mourn theory is to assume a certain stance toward as well as a definition of it.[7] If theory means poststructuralism(s) or all contemporary movements and schools or postmodern discourse, then we can project a historical passing, an end. Yet certain features of such theory will no doubt live on as, for instance, the deconstruction of binary concepts, interdisciplinary writings, and the critique of discriminatory gender and race conventions. Such talk about the passing of theory contains a disguised wish among some for its demise and, among others, a nostalgic lament about heady, intoxicating earlier days. End-of-theory sentiments arose, in fact, very early in the contemporary period: when the classical Enlightenment project of theory culminated in Frye's synoptic *Anatomy of Criticism*; when a bit later an array of new schools and movements were ascendant over formalism; then when French poststructuralism totally overwhelmed formalism; again when poststructuralism was displaced by cultural studies; and now when cultural studies, in its exemplary 1970s British form as opposed to its later, disaggregated North American version, projects in retrospect a comparatively coherent politics and project. Mourning theory expresses both a defense of certain earlier instantiations of it and, given current anxieties about an uncertain future, a longing for better times.

It is worth considering for a moment the notion of ends. The word has numerous connotations: withering, eclipse; fullness; closure, termination, catastrophe, death; turning or stopping points; goals and

11

targets. It summons an array of phenomena: finitude, beginnings and middles, expected change, nostalgia, mourning. It suggests remains, revenants, immortality. When ends designates regulated or calculated passing, it evokes cyclical patterns as well as shelf life, fusing historiography and fashion. Fashion itself brings to mind boredom, opportunism, mutability, superficiality. Ends, like origins, appear multiple and complex, which is the situation with "theory ends."

The past of theory demonstrates that theory has a future. Its long history, in its current telling, extends from the pre-Socratics through the lengthy Middle Ages; from the Renaissance, Enlightenment, and Romantic epochs to the Victorian, modern, and postmodern eras. These periods, of course, are regularly reconfigured in the light of new findings and pressing concerns. But neither the history of theoretical concepts, problems, and debates nor the search for effective methods and pragmatic protocols nor the influence of perennial theory texts nor the borrowing from neighboring fields nor the critique of the status quo seems likely to disappear. Like a riverbed, theory changes yet abides.

In its most colloquial sense, everyone has a theory, even if unconsciously held. Defined in this way, there can be no passing of theory *tout court*, only a loss of separate identity, an eclipse of certain functions, a reconfiguration or renaming. That is what is occurring at present.

Perhaps the main question today is, Where in the schools and universities of the future will literary and cultural theory be housed and studied? Under what conditions? How much? How widely? In most or just a few higher education humanities departments? In general education, introductory, or advanced theory courses? These questions raise the broader question of the future of the university. Will academic corporatization, with its addiction to casualized labor and its disinterest in humanities education, effectively reduce theory teaching, along with the venerable corps of tenured full-time faculty members to a mere shell of its former self?[8] Could expanding service teaching of the arts and humanities fully subordinate the research mission and its commitment to theory? Conversely, is it possible that emerging interdisciplinary formations might further disseminate theory? Even if passed and mourned, wouldn't theory return like a ghost in unexpected forms?

The theory market plays a role in this account. Such a thing hardly existed, at least in North America, before the 1970s. But the job market for theory expanded very dramatically from the early 1980s to the early 1990s, with many academic jobs going to theorists (labeled as such), especially in English and comparative literature programs. After that, the demand for theory diminished compared with that for other specialties in literature, language, and rhetoric. It appears to have remained steadily at the level of such premodern historical periods as eighteenth-century literature. However, a large number of jobs during recent years list theory as a second or preferred strength. That need provides openings to employment. More telling still is the role theory has come to play in research and publication. In most specialties, it is difficult to publish without some sort of informed theoretical orientation in use and on display. As a result, there are innumerable scholars not labeled theorists who know and use theory in their published work and in their teaching. So the market for theory is a matter not simply of designated specialists and specialty jobs but more or less the whole profession. Publication and also hiring are linked with theory across many specialties. It has been this way for a quarter century. The institutionalization of theory explains why it is sometimes regarded as a new orthodoxy, although there are so many different kinds and contentious factions that it is difficult to picture theory convincingly as one united or unifying, not to say stifling, force. The consecration of theory on the job market helps ensure a future.

Not surprisingly, fin-de-siècle moments prompt retrospection. Gains and losses are reckoned, futures solicited. For example, theory anthologies of recent years like the *Norton Anthology of Theory and Criticism* (2001) exhibit a retrospective tenor, displaying in bulky form and apparatus a full lineage for theory. All this reckoning entails the work of defense, consolidation, monumentalization. It puts on display Theory Incorporated, a holding company but a company with an eye toward a future of widely scattered franchise operations. Fashion and market models have sprung to the fore from the anxious unconscious of late capitalist times. Theory appears a niche market with fashions coming and going. Graduate students, in particular, wonder and frequently ask, Who is in? Who is out? What are the latest trends?

Causerie. Some theory brokers say new historicism, others proclaim cultural studies to be running out of energy. Yet other observers say the high times of US and UK theory – that is, the 1970s and 1980s and their legacies – are passing away and moving offshore. Belletrism is returning. Queer theory has now gone mainstream. Postcolonial theory is past its prime. Critical race theory definitely has legs.

Such speculations, reductions, preludes to calculated investments and disinvestments, reify and commodify theory, which is no surprise. It is how academic business is handled in our time of free-market capitalism. In this context, there will be and must be discussions of passing, mourning, the day after, the end, finitude. Indeed, there will be talk of shelf life, marketability, boom–bust cycles, new developments, the latest wave. The consumerist unconscious of the times calls forth such discourse.

Theory is part of its time. For example, the American New Criticism of the middle third of the twentieth century harmonized with the emergence of expanded higher education during its Keynesian era of big business+big labor+big government, mass media, the incorporation of modernist avant-gardes, large powerful political parties, and the coherent nuclear family. The poststructuralism of the later twentieth century was consonant with the spread of the disaggregated multiversity form and the rise of neoliberal capitalism, with its programs of minimal government+deregulation+deunionization, media proliferation, numerous reformist new social movements, and the flexibilization of monogamy. The cultural studies of recent years suits the stepped-up disorganization of higher education and growing globalization, characterized by dismantling governments, temped and insecure labor, mobile transnational businesses, the vulnerable single-headed family, proliferating yet conglomerated media, ubiquitous popular culture disseminated on a 24/7 basis, and literatures globalized (Anglophone, Francophone, Hispanophone, Sinophone, etc.).[9]

Theory Ends

Theory reflects its time and, while criticizing or sometimes ignoring or not analyzing, responds to the forces at play. The recent replacement of the vanguardist schools–and–movements paradigm of modern and contemporary theory by the rhizomatous studies model of the post–Cold War era foregrounds simultaneously three such forces: the rapid dedepartmentalization of knowledge and research; the collapse of the Enlightenment goal of maximum autonomy of spheres; and the niche marketization of all research areas now scrambling for publicity, funding, and legitimacy in neo-Darwinian struggles for survival and a piece of the future. Yet the shifts from high theory to posttheory to vernacular theory show theory not as moribund but, on the contrary, in a new viral form responsive to its time and place, materially engaged, socially symptomatic, critical, opportunistic, a changeling.

2

Teaching Theory Now

The teaching of contemporary literary and cultural theory particularly in the American university has been explicitly and increasingly caught up in politics. It was during the 1980s that conservative attacks like William Bennett's *To Reclaim a Legacy* and Allan Bloom's notorious *The Closing of the American Mind* began to defend vigorously the canon of great works against the purported corrupting influences both of popular culture and of nihilistic, usually foreign, theory. While this strand of the culture wars has ebbed and flowed over the decades, it continues into the new century, for example, with the publication of David Horowitz's *The Professors: The 101 Most Dangerous Academics in America* (2006). This work names names, and it speculates there are tens of thousands of "dangerous professors." Most are melodramatically associated with "ideological fields like women's studies, African American studies, gay and lesbian studies, postcolonial studies, queer studies, whiteness studies, and cultural studies."[1] What is wrong with such recent theory, according to this paleoconservative view, is not only that it corrupts the young and undermines patriotism, but that it questions traditional notions of scholarly disinterest, objectivity, and neutrality as well as standards of good professional methodology, conduct, and integrity.

When I started to teach theory in the 1970s, it was entangled with politics, although at that time it had much more of an internal configuration than the external framing of the later culture wars. Politics then took various and sundry forms such as Marxism versus formalism, radical versus liberal feminism, pan-African versus nationalist black aesthetics, literary structuralism versus contending extrinsically oriented criticisms, left versus right poststructuralism. Even though these theoretical camps were not disconnected from worldly politics, they often staged their disputes intramurally, appearing socially disengaged and isolated behind ivy-covered walls. This condition led to many calls during the 1980s and 1990s for the rebirth of the public intellectual, a figure for actively engaging with the world and especially for responding to the mounting conservative attacks against theory and the corruption of the university.

It was in this fin-de-siècle context that critical pedagogy, which derived from Paolo Freire's *Pedagogy of the Oppressed* and the broad New Left, gained a wide audience, as did the fair-minded liberal tactic of "teaching the conflicts" ably advocated by Gerald Graff.[2] Foremost among the conflicts of the time were the debates, still going today, surrounding multiculturalism. These invariably took up the conditions of black, brown, red, and yellow people; the related diasporas, colonialisms, imperialisms; and the need for new accounts of minorities constructed from below and from the margins.

But no sketch of the context for teaching theory and literary and cultural studies today could be complete without emphasizing the situation of academic labor. I am referring to the restructuring of the professoriate notably in the US since the 1970s, which involves the overproduction of Ph.D.s, the doubling of the time to earn the Ph.D. degree (currently nine years following the B.A.), the increasing use of cheap and insecure (nontenured) casual labor, and the growing number of unionization drives by graduate students and faculty. All this forms part of the framework for theory teaching in these times, as is elaborated in chapter 6.

In this chapter I address six key questions concerning theory teaching now. How does and should theory factor into the curriculum of the university literature major? What are the main goals for teaching theory? In what ways should one respond to opponents of theory and its teaching at institutions of higher education? What is the relationship between literary and critical theory and cultural

17

studies? What role does poststructuralism currently play in the teaching of theory? What is the future of theory in higher education?

How does and should theory factor into the curriculum of the university literature major today? Most North American literature students are required to complete one or two introductory theory courses during their sequence of eight to ten courses. At my institution, a typical large US state university, undergraduate students take both Introduction to Critical Reading and Writing and Introduction to Literary and Cultural Studies. They can supplement these two with optional offerings. One that I regularly teach, for example, is Issues in Cultural Studies. There are numerous anthologies, readers, guide books, and glossaries for all such theory courses, whether beginning or advanced, to help faculty and students. I expect something resembling this institutionalization of theory to continue into the foreseeable future. In this way students gain necessary knowledge of the premises and practices of literary formalism, psychoanalysis, feminism, poststructuralism, Marxism, new historicism, etc. as well as awareness of the history of thinking about literature from Plato and Aristotle to Bourdieu and Butler.

What is less obvious and perhaps more important is the incalculable theory teaching that happens in the other courses taken by literature majors, ranging from ancient and medieval literature up to the present. I have in mind, for instance, the new feminist and queer perspectives on Shakespeare and Renaissance drama; critiques of modernization relating to eighteenth- and nineteenth-century fiction; the emergence of globalized Anglophone literatures and postcolonial theories; the relevance of the deconstruction of the human subject and the rise of contemporary cyberpunk and interactive fictions. But I also have in mind the close reading of the lyric poem in the old ingrained early postwar formalist manner and the still more venerable commonsense historicization and moralization of literary settings, characters, themes, and authors. Such unprogrammed encounters with theory in every classroom and in all reading and writing assignments constitute a second front of theory teaching in the always important informal curriculum. My point here is that in the multitude of syllabi, one-off course packs, and impromptu as well as planned course discussions, theory shows itself more a part of the atmosphere than simply a discrete well-packaged subdiscipline or specialty contained in one or two introductory courses.

About the goals of teaching theory, certain well-recognized general aims remain essential. These include teaching students to think and read critically; to write well; to master technical terms and knowledge; to grapple with canonical texts, figures, and traditions; and to contextualize materials historically. This is a matter of discipline in several senses: as a prescribed body of knowledge; as training in required skills; as good professional practice.

Grading, exams, and recommendation letters come in here. Students are required to be on time with assignments and class attendance. They are expected to exhibit good manners in the conventional social and professional senses. As everyone knows, the teaching profession is integrated into bureaucracies and ideological state apparatuses. That was made memorably clear three decades ago by Richard Ohmann's *English in America* and contemporaneous works by Bourdieu, particularly his co-authored *Reproduction in Education, Society and Culture.*[3] Not surprisingly, professors sometimes work against the grain, uncomfortable teaching certain requirements of the reigning social order and discipline. But there is no way to inventory the innumerable modes of resistance, often spontaneous, singular, local.

The teaching goals specific to literary theory are for me probably best summarized by exploring in the classroom the following repertoire of fundamental questions: What is literature? Who defines it? In what ways? How is it produced, disseminated, used, evaluated? What are the protocols of interpretation? How and why do the definitions, roles, and social positions of author, reader, and literary genre change? What institutions are involved in literature and literary teaching? Do past answers to such questions have currency today? For cultural theory courses or modules, we can change the word literature here to culture. At the risk of being formulaic, to theorize characteristically entails asking fundamental questions, scrutinizing answers, and seeking new, often defamiliarized, understandings, concepts, practices. It takes place within but it is not limited to disciplinary frameworks.

Given the improvisational performative dimensions of classroom teaching, there exist, of course, elements of potential fun and danger, of risk, for all teaching, but perhaps more so for contemporary theory teaching with its skeptical historicist disposition, penchant for speculation, and antinomian drift. In this connection, most teachers today no doubt increasingly feel themselves part of the entertainment industry rather like standup comedians or talking heads on television. Media values during our postmodern times have seeped into numerous previously autonomous domains. Nowadays the classroom is a commercialized as well as a surveilled public space.

Full-time tenure-track faculty are accountable at US institutions. That turns out to play a considerable role in shaping course goals. Like many workers today, professors receive regular multifaceted formal evaluation and supervision. To begin with, North American students in each course typically complete end-of-semester rating sheets, responding numerically and in prose to a dozen or more questions about teaching. The anonymous results are quantified and compared with a statistical group such as all literature or all arts and sciences professors, using standard deviations and median scores. Also there are annual evaluations of each professor's teaching, research, and service by departmental administrators and/or senior faculty. Moreover, junior faculty undergo periodic progress-to-tenure reviews as well as the tenure review itself, the latter often involving anywhere from five to twelve outside evaluators in addition to departmental colleagues. More and more senior professors face periodic post-tenure review. I had one following five years of tenured service, and every five years since. Among other things, I am required to project ahead and plan for five years and to look back and self-evaluate the past five years. That kind of extensive formal ten-year examination of the professional self is increasingly common. It is worth underlining here two conflicting modes of evaluation, reflecting contending styles of modern management (scientific and humanistic), with the quantitative in the ascendancy. Casual faculty receive less evaluation, sometimes none. But we are all on stage and accountable. It is in large part a numbers game.

During spring the Provost at my university requires each faculty member to hand in a one-page mini-vita recording accomplishments in teaching, research, and service for the prior calendar year. The department chair and two elected senior faculty then assign a grade in each category, ranging from zero to five, worked out to the second decimal point. So a faculty member might receive a 3.75 in teaching, 4.50 in service, and 4.10 in research. The annual evaluation sheet also lately totals up three-year rolling averages in each category plus composite averages for each year and for three years, all worked out to the second decimal point. My composite for last year was 4.50 and for the past three years 4.69. This kind of severe mathematical reduction in the interest of institutional accounting would, no doubt, give Pythagoras himself pause. It plays havoc with the self-image of would-be independent, not to mention rebel and bohemian professors. It is not just that it affects faculty annual raises and sense of self-worth as well as future strategies for career success, but it privileges the short term and speed-up. (Faculty had to campaign for the three-year averages.) Ten-year scholarly projects appear old-fashioned, incalculable, despite the impression of post-tenure reviews. In much post-industrial capitalist work, education included, productivity must be quantifiable, copious, rapid.

This whole apparatus of necessary and often useful accountability affects teaching goals. At various times I, like others, have tailored my teaching to discard low-scoring activities, to increase high-scoring practices, to maximize short-term returns. Such behavior is, I believe, second nature now to contemporary American professors, shaping all aspects of teaching, including theory teaching and its goals, for good and ill.

How does one respond to the main opponents of theory and its teaching in institutions of higher education? There are several justifications and refutations worth highlighting. To start with, history of theory teaches the great tradition, with its foundational figures and texts from Plato's *Republic* and Aristotle's *Poetics* to Bloom's *The Anxiety of Influence*, Gilbert and Gubar's *Madwoman in the Attic*, and

21

Said's *Culture and Imperialism*. In addition, it teaches canonical answers to perennial questions about literature and culture such as the place of censorship, the elements of genre, the dynamics of tradition and influence, the role of madness in the arts, the social mission of literary education. Theory teaches not only cultural history and literary appreciation, but critical reading and self-reflexively the historical development of critical reading. Now to the complaint, often seeming hysterical, that theory students are taken away from studying literature and the canonical texts, my experience and empirical studies undertaken by the Modern Language Association of America have demonstrated that simply is not the case.[4] Here I would recall also what Frye in *Anatomy of Criticism* pointed out: literature majors study criticism not literature, with the latter taken up by creative writers.[5] As concerns contemporary theory, in particular, from formalism, structuralism, and new strands of psychoanalysis and Marxism to reader-response criticism, deconstruction, new historicism, postcolonial studies, and queer theory, all these movements and schools have happened and cannot be ignored. Of course, they should be evaluated and criticized where necessary. Programs of literary and cultural study are obliged to teach developments in recent professional history, their roots, mechanisms, conflicts.

Angry charges of partisanship and classroom advocacy invariably arise in attacks upon the teaching of contemporary theory. The time-tested way to avoid such problems is to teach all schools of criticism as optional points of view and reading strategies – the so-called approaches method. That is the way I learned theory in the 1960s. The Marxist approach, the formalist approach, the psychological approach – take your pick. Whatever critical methodology works is fine. The proof is in the pudding: outcomes matter uppermost. Practical criticism is what is important after all. One variation on this way of handling the issue is for the teacher to be studiously neutral, teaching what has happened and how the different methods operate. Teach the conflicts and stay out of it.

It was Robert Scholes, however, who noted in *Textual Power* that critical reading, that is, reading against the grain as distinct from both explanatory and sympathetic textual interpretation, depends on communal standpoint.[6] One undertakes critique, Marxist, feminist, Christian, conservative, etc., as a member of a group. Everybody stands somewhere whether he or she realizes it or not. This standpoint epistemology, characteristic of our postmodern posthumanist times, challenges all calls for neutrality. It also undermines the pragmatic methodologization of critical schools and movements which transforms beliefs and perspectives into convenient flexible tools, into approaches. For example, feminist theory for many women is not one approach selected among many, but an existential perspective built out of painful lived experience. Some of the best teachers are extreme in their beliefs. So advocacy yes, but indoctrination no.[7] Compulsory objectivity and obligatory critical disinterest, sacred cows of many a theory opponent, often mask blind spots, racial and gender privileges, nationalistic mindsets, and prejudices.

This is a good place to address the question of the relationship between literary and critical theory and cultural studies. Because disciplines bear distinct and perdurable national frameworks as well as national traditions, the position of cultural studies vis-à-vis literary theory differs in Australia, Canada, the United Kingdom, the United States, etc. Consider the place of cultural studies, for instance, in the UK, which is markedly different from the US. The British history famously goes back to the 1950s works of Hoggart, Williams, Hall, and the slightly later Centre for Contemporary Cultural Studies at the University of Birmingham (1960s–1980s). By the mid-1980s the spread of cultural studies as a breakaway distinct discipline across the UK academic world appeared an accomplished fact. This is the point at which US cultural studies begins. I have told this story elsewhere so I won't repeat it here.[8] Now looking back several decades, I can summarize the most obvious differences by saying that early cultural studies in the UK was a school, if not a coterie, while in the US it was an amorphous movement, lacking consensus on politics as well as essential traditions. By the dawn of the twenty-first century, even though US cultural studies had seeped into many humanistic and social scientific disciplines, but in unequal and

23

singular ways, it did not become a separate discipline. Where it is not simply cast as one methodology among others today, US cultural studies takes the peculiar form of a small wing, camp, or tendency inside traditional fields such as anthropology, communication studies, comparative literature, English, political science, and sociology. So do not go looking for departments of cultural studies on US campuses. Needless to say, the role of theory in this situation is quite complex, requiring a discipline-by-discipline account.

When, for example, I worked as a professor in the Department of English at Purdue University, it was in the late 1990s that a handful of faculty and graduate students managed to establish within that unit a graduate program in Theory and Cultural Studies (TCS). The preexisting semiautonomous programs inside that large department included Creative Writing, English as a Second Language, English Linguistics, English Education, Literary Studies, and Rhetoric and Composition. Each offered precedents and program models for TCS. The formation of a parallel semiautonomous TCS entailed a repackaging of existing graduate courses, including both the three long-standing graduate courses in the history of theory (Plato to Kant; Wordsworth to Eliot; Contemporary Schools and Movements) and the usual variable topics seminars in theory. In the context of such repackagings, Wollstonecraft's *A Vindication of the Rights of Woman*, Arnold's *Culture and Anarchy*, Marx's previously ignored writings on commodification in *Capital*, and the Frankfurt school's works on culture (especially those by Adorno and Benjamin) gained pride of place in the history of literary theory courses. Theory went cultural. Contemporary critical theory offerings, not surprisingly, accorded increased room to culturally oriented poststructuralists (notably Althusser, Bourdieu, Foucault) and to Birmingham scholars like Hall, Hebdige, and McRobbie. While there is a distinct cultural studies theory course imaginable and on offer here and there, cultural studies theory is usually embedded into literary and critical theory courses in English departments. In other words, cultural studies for US literary theory is commonly treated as one more school or movement like reader-response theory, new historicism, ethnic criticism, queer theory, etc. It is one among many other approaches. In the case of the TCS program, cultural studies was caught – symptomatically so – between its tendency to be a new discipline or, less ambitiously, a semiautonomous subfield and its sacred obligations to the overarching goals of literary and rhetorical education within the US English department and discipline.

There are yet further wrinkles in this account. Cultural studies in the US is for literary and cultural theory not only a methodology or an approach as well as a recent movement, but, significantly, a paradigm. So there are five faces of American cultural studies: approach or method; school or movement; disciplinary wing or tendency; new discipline or department; and main paradigm of research within a department. Starting in the 1990s and up to the present, cultural studies in English departments occupies a central position as did formalism/New Criticism from the 1940s to the1960s and poststructuralism from the 1970s to the 1980s. It is the dominant model of research and scholarship in a field of contenders, only vastly more heterogeneous than its two immediate forerunners. This cultural studies consists of several dozen semi-autonomous areas of research and study such as, to repeat the standard list, body studies, indigenous studies, institutional studies, material culture studies, media studies, popular culture studies, porn studies, subculture studies, trauma studies, whiteness studies, working-class studies, etc. While some resist incorporation, most scholars in these subfields consider themselves to be part of cultural studies. That is the ruling paradigm.

Consequently, when I teach an undergraduate course on Issues in Cultural Studies in the English department, I offer a half dozen modules on variable topics focusing upon contemporary US "literary" matters. They range from female body images in advertising discourses (body studies) and in pulp fictions (popular culture studies) to the activities of bookstores (institutional studies) to the phenomena of slam poetry (media studies) to the upsurge of white trash literature and television shows (working-class and whiteness studies). This is a kind of literary theory teaching that I could not have imagined when I started out in the 1970s as a professor of English. Nor could I have foreseen, being under the sway of formalism then, the types of critical

25

theories and practices brought to bear now. These include institutional analysis and ideology critique that systematically attend to the circuits of cultural production, distribution, and consumption, plus matters of race, class, gender, and national identity (all essential elements of analysis for the reigning cultural studies paradigm).

However odd, uncomfortable, and fleeting a situation it may be, cultural studies has recently become an orthodoxy of sorts in US English departments. At the same time it retains much of its socially critical edge and its links with antinomian critical theory. Conservative critics of cultural studies and its subdivisions, as a result, regard themselves very self-righteously as an embattled minority, a heterodoxy, defending the great tradition and objective scholarship against popular culture and the debased new postmodern discipline of cultural studies purportedly given over *in toto* to theory, multiculturalism, political correctness, and classroom advocacy. Those are main battle lines for classroom teachers in the early twenty-first century.

On the question of what role poststructuralism currently plays in teaching theory, I would say without fear of contradiction that it is ubiquitous and indispensable, yet its prominence has receded since the late 1980s. Whether one is thinking of contemporary literary theory, critical theory, cultural theory, or theory in general, several handfuls of poststructuralist concepts form part of the lexicon of key terms as, for example, docile body, cultural capital, male gaze, heteroglossia, ideological state apparatus, the imaginary, floating signifier, intertextuality, deconstruction, subject-in-process, surveillance society, etc. These regularly show up in glossaries, of course. They remain productive critical and speculative instruments in the classroom. The teaching of the major figures and texts of poststructuralism has been more or less standardized by now, as a review of theory anthologies and readers reveals. There is a well-sifted recurring body of poststructuralist texts from Althusser, Barthes, Baudrillard, Bourdieu, Cixous, Deleuze, Derrida, Foucault, Irigaray, Kristeva, Lacan, etc. When I and the five editors of the *Norton Anthology of Theory and Criticism* made our poststructuralist selections, there was little difficulty in choosing teachable as well as rewarding and influential texts.[9] The real challenge was finding new undiscovered gems such as some of the lesser-known essays of Barthes's *Mythologies* or overlooked chapters in Kristeva's *Revolution in Poetic Language*. Even though certain poststructuralists are legendarily difficult like Derrida, Lacan, and second-generation ones like Bhabha and Butler, there are nowadays ways and aids to contextualize and set up their works, making them meaningful to literature majors whether advanced or beginners.

Yet there are vexing problems of naturalization, recuperation, canonization, and taming, pertaining as much to postmodern post-structuralist texts as to earlier avant-garde modernist works. Just the same, there seem regularly and surprisingly to be new things to find in previous texts. I am thinking of the indigestible, the undiscovered, the unseen, the contradiction, the gap, the new context or lens, not to mention the new text. Many of Foucault's lectures have yet to see print in English. The three dozen books from Derrida's last 15 years have hardly been opened, much less digested for pedagogy. I believe there are futures for poststructuralism beyond mechanical repetitions and calcifications.

For me a productive role for poststructuralism today lies not only in its inventive concepts and its continuing position as useful target and revealing scapegoat, but in its openness to external critique and self-critique. Based on my experience, a classroom teacher can inter-rogate the standard poststructuralist works to good effect. For instance, many poststructuralist texts overplay the suffocating seamlessness of social systems, appearing blind to resistance and alternatives. That pertains to Foucault's panoptic society, Althusser's ideological state apparatuses, Derrida's logocentrism, and Bourdieu's habitus. But within poststructuralist theory there are key texts giving voice to resistance. Here is where enter, for example, de Certeau's famous resisting practices of everyday life; Deleuze and Guattari's nomads and schizos pioneering lines of flight and deterritorializations; Cixous's disruptive *écriture féminine*; Kristeva's modernist revolution in poetic language; the creative role accorded by Said against Foucault to certain rare independent thinkers of orientalism; and Barthes's imaginative and self-indulgent writerly readers. Each of these forms of resistance against specific social institutions and oppressive practices is itself open to critique. So there is a rich body of material here for current and future theory that opens to account the strengths and weaknesses of poststructuralism.

What, speaking very broadly, now, is the future of theory teaching in higher education? First and foremost, theory is an established element of programs in literary study and cultural studies not just in North America but elsewhere, to be sure. It is increasingly recognized and accredited across the arts, humanities, social sciences, and professions (particularly law). And significantly, it is studied more and more around the globe, notably in Central and Northern Europe and in East Asia. There lies a substantial future.

Sooner or later, however, theory, especially the history of theory and its teaching, must take on non-European traditions stemming from Arabic, Chinese, Indian, Japanese, and other sources. So right there both in materials and in outreach rests another future for theory.

The dissemination of theory through innumerable academic specialties, subspecialties, areas, periods, disciplines, and national contexts continues apace. Here and there it loses its distinct identity through grafting and incorporation. The tendency for almost everyone, it seems, particularly in US literary and cultural studies, to see themselves as having and doing theory, which marks a certain annexation and weakening of its identity, can be anticipated to continue. Paradoxically, this accounts for the diminution in the job market for theorists since the high watermark of the 1980s while bearing witness to an unequivocal, though ambiguous, triumph. Since just about everyone, whether scholar of medieval, Renaissance, Enlightenment, or modern literary culture, does theory of some sort in the US, there appears little reason to secure the services of scholars doing full-time stand-alone theory. Area and period specialists can teach theory as need be and on the side so to speak. What this comes down to is the reassertion of the powerful modern (pre-postmodern) matrix of scholarship where recognized periods and genre hierarchies set within clear and certain national contexts form the rigid infrastructure and value system of the arts and humanities. In this scenario, theory, like textual bibliography and linguistics, is a handmaiden in service to aesthetic analysis, historical investigation, cultural critique. It appears a historical anomaly on its way out. So it is that US doctoral students wanting to specialize in theory nowadays strategically adopt a secondary recognized literary area, usually contemporary American fiction or poetry, as a way to put on a traditional face in order to improve their chances in a long-overcrowded job market. For many young theorists, theory in disguise and in the backseat is the future.

Given the growing number of segments as well as faultlines running through the domain of theory, it is no surprise that it increasingly takes the form of semi-autonomous enclaves. Proliferation generates disaggregation. Overviews have become harder to draw. Since the late 1990s, it has seemed impossible to map the world of theory, with its lengthening list of "studies" areas. Under such conditions, teaching is very much a matter of sampling and mixing and matching. Which constitutes a certain future for theory teaching.

This is a good spot, now at the close of the discussion, to summon up the teaching body and persona performing in front of captive students. There is, to begin with, the matter of deportment and its many implications. In my personal case I would say my daily suits and often ties, for instance, sometimes act as camouflage, conservative cover for irreverent interrogations of the status quo. I like to think so. Twelve years of Catholic school and two years in a Merchant Marine academy, all in uniform with tie, mean I don't squirm and yank at the collar. I pass comfortably. Fashion speaks. My public voice, exercised daily in order to be deep, clear, loud, and free of my "wretched" New York dialect, exudes white male authority but is softened for other effects. The message is: here stands professorial authority, confident, self-assured, yet enthusiastically, sometimes corrosively, open-minded. The doctored voice is a main instrument of teaching.

For teachers there is always the background of syllabi, mandatory course plans, sequenced modules, coverage of material, legal requirements, calls to duty as well as regimented seats, class times, expected attendance, grades, docile bodies, official records, very bright lights.

The two main temptations of classroom teaching from time immemorial have been "turkey stuffing" and "cruising." I mean lecturing and dialogue, drifting, excursions into unplanned spaces. The rigid body and the body in motion. The moments of getting lost, of rifts, of roaming take place within the larger context of well-designed courses and curricula. Such moments gravitate toward questions, contradictions, paradoxes, countercurrents. In my experience it is always best to be on the lookout for these opportunities rather than leaving them to pure chance. Being raised on the South Shore of Long Island, my favorite sport has long been body surfing in the Atlantic Ocean. While there is inevitably a rhythm to the waves, the odd ones, slightly askew, often deliver the best rides, provided the prevailing currents and undercurrents line up just right. Catching a wave looks like luck, and it is, but it depends on attentiveness, judgment, opportunism, a body positioned in a certain way open to the most immediate future. Body work, I know, plays out differently for women and for minority teachers.

Anyone who has looked into "futures" on today's financial markets realizes not only that they are highly risky instruments, but that they focus on short-term performance, one year or less. You put up a little money (a small margin) and open a future position, choosing either to speculate on an increasing market or to hedge on a declining market for, say, oil, coffee, sugar, or some other asset. On any day during the term of the brief contract, you can estimate the fair value of your futures asset. (There is a standard calculation which takes into account average rate of profit, prevailing interest rates, current price of the asset in question, and the terms of your contract). If you choose, you can close out your position at any time. In our current neoliberal capitalist milieu, an era of fast turnovers and casino sensibilities, "futures" signify quick gains made off growth or decline. No matter which. It goes without saying that investors do not generally produce assets, rather they speculate on them. Not surprisingly, there is an academic futures market in theory, including the history of theory.

The theory futures market is more volatile than the markets, for instance, in Renaissance or Enlightenment research and scholarship.[10]

30

Academics, whether theorists or not, but especially up-and-coming young scholars, will calculate on any given day how the market looks for new historicism, feminist theory, poststructuralism, cultural studies, Marxism, new formalisms, postcolonial theory, etc. Intellectuals today operate in a world of markets. You can close out or open a position on any theory at any moment. Personally, I am regularly asked by students, faculty, and others about theory and cultural studies: whether to buy, sell, or hold and in just those terms. People want to know very badly what is the latest thing. Without being coy, I remain wary of my role as futures advisor for potential theory investors, including bemused professional onlookers. In the latter category I have in mind higher education journalists, humanities deans, book publishers, and journal editors. I work for them too. My closing point: there is a future in theory futures.

3

Applied Theory

In the wake of 1970s reader–response criticism, especially, theory often came to mean a toolbox of interpretive strategies employed by distinct groups such as particular critical schools, movements, or subcultures. This is what I am calling in chapter 3 applied theory. As the premises and protocols of applied theory have multiplied during the postmodern period from the 1970s onwards, reading has entered a state of disorganization, meaning proliferation, pluralization, and flexibilization.[1] In the US this transformation has come about in three waves. During the 1950s the academic literary reading regime consisted of a mildly capacious dominant formalism challenged, sometimes vigorously, by various myth critics, social critics, and a few philologists and phenomenologists. By the late 1970s the situation had altered noticeably with the rise to prominence of a multifaceted poststructuralism that permeated and energized, to one degree or another, contending reading formations, including Marxism, feminism, reception theory, ethnic aesthetics (with African American in the vanguard), and new historicism. By the early 1990s cultural studies had become the dominant reading paradigm flanked by the closely related satellite, yet sometimes separatist projects of both queer and postcolonial theory as well as Asian, Hispanic, and Native American studies.[2] During the past decade, however, a few dozen subfields of cultural studies have emerged as semiautonomous, such as trauma studies, environmental studies, disability studies, body studies, most having developed distinct reading premises and protocols. There are now many brands of applied theory.

It is worth remembering that when Stanley Fish famously introduced the explosive flexibilizing idea of contending "interpretive communities," he was depicting 1970s realities, that is, a limited array of academic readers adhering to different internally consistent interpretive strategies and charters.[3] Tellingly, he exhibited at the time no interest in class or gender dynamics among his supposed equals, nor in nonacademic subcultural readers, nor in the rabble of textual poachers who mix and match protocols in a spontaneous manner typical of rock critics, cartoonists, and later maverick bloggers. Fish's readers were professional exegetes, university specialists employing productive routines and special conventions. Nowhere considered among his interpretive communities were common readers (a populist myth arguably) nor deviant readers nor organic intellectuals nor consumers of popular culture texts, all of whom operate outside consecrated academic spaces and employ nonelite practices. Professionalism constituted and constrained realities then. But with the development of cultural studies in the 1980s and thereafter, such vernacular readers have been increasingly visible and acknowledged, touted often for their resisting agency, imagination, and critical independence.

One especially significant realm for the contemporary disaggregation of applied theory explored by cultural studies literary researchers involves the scholarly documentation and analysis of vernacular reading communities and conventions. Here I have uppermost in mind ethnographically framed studies of the reading practices of popular culture fans occupying distinct subcultures. They range from women fans of romance fiction famously studied by Janice Radway to media fans of television series by Henry Jenkins to fans of pop music by Thomas McLaughlin. The main argument of these three representative studies, which I examine in the first two-thirds of this chapter, is that subalterns not only decode but also talk back and often write back in distinctive nonacademic ways. This is so, in part, by virtue of street smarts, but in large part through the fans' memberships in subcultures and nonhegemonic groups that involve affiliations along various lines of gender, class, sexuality, race, and national identification.

The growing awareness about different interpretive communities of vernacular as well as academic readers has gradually opened to question the longstanding pedagogical goal of teaching critical reading to university students. Recently, Michael Warner among others has addressed this topic pointedly by reconsidering the uniform premises of the Enlightenment project of critical reading. He projects its demise, though not without mixed feelings. In the closing third of the chapter, I discuss how things stand today, and should stand, with the teaching of reading, in particular with the related practices of close reading, ideology critique, and cultural critique, none of which I am willing to scrap.

In the introduction to her landmark book, *Reading the Romance*, Janice Radway rightly points out that her US-centered research parallels the celebrated ethnographies of subcultures undertaken in the 1970s and 1980s at the pioneering Birmingham Centre for Contemporary Cultural Studies. The membership of the interpretive community of Radway's romance readers consists of 42 mostly lower middle-class housewives living in a Midwestern suburb. They are brought together by Radway and one of their number who works in a shopping mall chain bookstore and writes a monthly newsletter rating and recommending new romance novels. By means of interviews, group discussions, and elaborate questionnaires, Radway isolates the complicated, conflicted web of these romance readers' complicities with and resisting tactics against the patriarchal order, with its hetero-sexual marriage and its ideology of romantic love. Significantly, they are nonfeminist women having a little or no higher education. Their reading practices reveal almost nothing in common with academic protocols of interpretation. This is a separate world of applied vernacular theory. They read rapidly, often skip to the end, pay no attention to style, ignore critical distance, identify strongly with characters (notably heroines), and care most about plot and its certainties. They share strong dislikes, meaning they have prescriptive criteria: no violent heroes, weak heroines, pornography, unhappy or ambiguous endings. They care nothing for original interpretations, rigorous argumentation, or exacting analyses of literary craftsmanship. They flagrantly violate the affective fallacy, being cooperative, appreciative, self-indulgent rather than self-conscious objective disinterested critical readers.

Radway offers a sympathetic, only mildly critical, account of this community of vernacular readers. She argues convincingly for subterranean aspects of North American romance fiction (1980s vintage), which, however, obviously champions traditional monogamous heterosexual courtship and marriage. The ideal relationship of mutual love and perfect union, repetitively portrayed and admittedly addictive for the community members, constitutes a compensatory fantasy and utopian form. It is set against the grimmer realities of contemporary marriage, where husbands are frequently nonexpressive, ungentle, and preoccupied with work and sports. Romance novels portray a new man, strong, successful, protective, communicative, and nurturing, who puts love first. Not insignificantly, the very opportunity of women to buy and read such fiction is regularly challenged by disapproving spouses and family members. That highlights the 24/7 on-call labor conditions of the traditional housewife whose rights to privacy, spending money, and leisure require constant struggle. In this context, the event of reading is itself an oppositional act, signifying liberation, however limited and contested.

Romance readers, like their heroines (their alter egos), are able, intelligent, independent, opposing oppression. This is Radway's main finding. They read for relaxation, escape, pleasure, restoration, and therapy, secondarily picking up knowledge as they go. Given the formulaic nature of the fiction, their activity is ritualistic: romance fans are obsessive, voracious readers by any measure. Radway provides copious evidence. They pay no attention to literary technique, aesthetic refinement, or disinterested reading tactics. They reread favorite novels, usually when depressed. Their interest in interpretation is limited to the hero's questionable motives at mid-course. Here is Radway on the reader of romance: "There is little need for that reader to attend to the nuances of any particular novel in order to understand the nature of the story. Her energy is reserved, therefore, for the more desirable activity of affective reaction rather than prematurely spent on the merely intermediary task of interpretation."[4] Romance reading ideally involves no work; it is an activity providing relaxation and pleasure. By academic standards, Radway's subjects are uncommon, not to say peculiar readers, definitely not critical or close readers in the usual senses.

It is easy enough to criticize such vernacular readers, as Radway gently does. She also criticizes the romance genre and quite rightly herself for paying no heed to race and class factors.[5] One can, in addition, find problems with the romance publishing industry and its manipulations, which Radway does in her opening chapter on institutional matrices. But the main impetus of cultural studies work on nonacademic vernacular reading is to document sympathetically, in general ethnographically, sometimes through participant observation, alternative modes of reading and subcultural interpretive communities. It is odd that Radway does not worry about her distance, that is, her experimental, affective, and socioeconomic removes from her subjects. Significantly, there is little or no explicit criticism from her of normative academic critical reading. Which is simply positioned as another and distant universe. She presumes while illustrating the disaggregation of contemporary applied theory.

In his book *Textual Poachers*, Henry Jenkins, unlike Radway, identifies himself as an avid fan and participant observer, not just a scholar, of an alternative interpretive community. In this case it is US-based media fan culture, a little understood or documented phenomenon. Educated middle-class and predominantly women, these fans are devoted to certain popular television series like *Star Trek*, *Quantum Leap*, *War of the Worlds*, *Beauty and the Beast*, and several dozen others, ranging across many genres. Strikingly different from the general television audience, the fans typically own copies of each show; know the series details; participate in regular club meetings, group viewings, and online discussion forums; attend fan conventions; and produce and enjoy fan newsletters, videos, artworks, and songs. Unlike the docile subjects of official fan organizations, these unofficial fans sometimes become unruly activists, mounting grassroots campaigns to defend shows against producers' and networks' decisions.

They are, stresses Jenkins, participants not spectators. They constitute an underground subculture. Here is how he portrays them in relation to the media conglomerates: "Like the poachers of old, fans operate from a position of cultural marginality and social weakness. Like other popular readers, fans lack direct access to the means of commercial cultural production and have only the most limited resources with which to influence entertainment industry's decisions. . . . Within the cultural economy, fans are peasants, not proprietors. . . . "[6]

While from a top-down point of view media fans are disempowered and weak, from Jenkins's alternative bottom-up cultural studies perspective they engage in creative resistance and enjoy considerable autonomy. This is most notable in their production, distribution, and consumption of zines. The broad category zines here includes newsletters containing commentary; anthologies of poems, stories, and novels; plus comic books, songbooks, cookbooks, and collected essays. Such fanzines focus on individual popular programs, although they occasionally derive from single fringe shows or generalist orientations. It is the zine, in this very broad sense, that foregrounds most memorably the independent creative and critical dimensions of media fandom.

One of the most significant aspects of media fandom is the practice of commentary, which ranges far and wide, especially in zines. Particularly noteworthy are the forms of fans' responsive rewriting. There are, for example, numerous stories, novels, videos, and other visual items that play variations on popular television series like *Star Trek*. Here fans critically and imaginatively transform characters, themes, and plots. At one point Jenkins codifies ten modes of such rewriting, including, to name just two, genre shifting (for instance, emphasis on the friendship of Kirk and Spock instead of space adventure) and eroticization (for example, fanciful homoerotic activities of Kirk and Spock rather than the usual respectful professional distance). Such home improvements by fans constitute new readings and critiques. In their applied theory, media fan critics, unlike academics, flagrantly refuse authorial authority, violate intellectual property (the sacred text), blur fact and fiction (just as they blur reading and writing), explicitly inject personal associations and values, and rework ideology. Unlike the private and evanescent critical perceptions spun off by innumerable consumers of popular culture, fan critics produce durable forms of reading and commentary through multifarious zine publications addressed to their communities.

There are three protocols of media fan reading and rewriting worthy of special mention as evidence that academics and fan critics employ parallel yet different interpretive tactics. First, fan commentary presupposes and requires familiarity not only with all series episodes, but with secondary sources such as, in this case, convention appearances, interviews, program guidelines (documents used by series writers), and earlier fan speculations. Jenkins dubs this the "meta-text," deeming it the foundation of fan expertise and discourse. Second, fan reading depends on tacit frames of reference, specifically ruling hypotheses about genre. While television series characteristic-ally mix traditional genres, as, for example, romance, action adventure, crime fighting, and utopian fiction, different fan segments choose a dominant form and use it to guide interpretation and assessment. This protocol accounts for differences of interpretation in a regulated way. Interpretative disputes involve less matters of personal taste than group consensus on genre expectations. Third, like academics, fans ask of a work "emotional realism," meaning plausibility, coherence, vraisemblance. Such realism, even in the case of aliens and space travel, derives from experience, common sense, and social norms.

Where the media fans most differ from academic readers is arguably the fanaticism entailed in the acquisition and display of the meta-text. Interestingly, however, there is little difference of expertise since both modes of reading require extensive knowledge. Another obvious difference is that media fans repudiate the high/low cultural divide, which academics, in fact, very rarely do. Finally, in their rereading fans are generally more compulsive, as attested to by the frequent comparisons of them to religious fanatics and hypersensitive scriptural exegetes.[7]

Jenkins touches on several related revealing topics, but only in passing. The matter of costume wearing at fan conventions, to begin with, suggests a particularly intense and embodied form of playful escape and fantasy. Is this a matter of a subset of fan interpreters who are too literal-minded? I would like to know what applied theorists are wearing and what that may signify. Jenkins does not say. Secondly, the phenomenon of the meta-text hints at hierarchy within fandom where tensions likely exist between masters and apprentices, not to mention less stark differences among knowledgeable fans. How are fan interpretive conflicts and differences in cultural capital handled? Jenkins does not address the issue. As a result, fan communities appear overly harmonious. Thirdly, the minority position of males within largely female media fandom deserves, I imagine, a separate treatment where formal reading protocols would doubtless be just one segment of a larger set of discursive practices, including gender-marked genres like gossip and pen names. How do things work for sub-subcultural male fans? Lastly, media fans are communal close readers, much more so than Radway's comparatively solitary and relaxed romance readers, yet there is in both instances an unselfconscious hobbyist dynamic of reading as leisure activity, escapism, and pleasurable consumerism. Can the standard cultural studies argument that popular culture contains hidden utopian moments and socially symptomatic compensations continue to serve as justification for serious engagement with it? Should Jenkins, and Radway too, be more critical of pleasure-seeking vernacular consumer-readers, despite such readers' diligence, imagination, and independence? Can case studies of applied theory, whether vernacular or academic, skirt such assessments?

Thomas McLaughlin's *Street Smarts and Critical Theory: Listening to the Vernacular* offers five case studies of vernacular as explicitly opposed to academic theorist-readers. The variegated cases examine in order (1) activist tracts by an anti-pornography Southern Christian minister; (2) zines from popular culture fans; (3) narratives of dramatic life changes by New Age authors; (4) apologias from people working in the advertising industry; and (5) testimonies by primary school language teachers enthusiastically converting from basal to whole language pedagogy. McLaughlin takes the contemporary deconstruction of the theory/practice binary as his starting point. He follows Stanley Fish: "Fish is right to identify theory as a practice among practices, with no privileged status."[8] He sees critical theory being done all around him in everyday life by ordinary people and engaged subjects as well as by academics. Theory for him means skeptical applied theory, that is, regular questioning of ruling assumptions, values, and operations carried out in specific interpretive situations. It entails interrogations of the status quo, proposals for alternatives, resistances to power. McLaughlin's work fruitfully extends US cultural studies' accounts of applied theory, although it has been overlooked.

Vernacular applied theory in McLaughlin's treatment stems from people who lack both power and academic language. It appears in a wide array of quotidian genres from gripes, jokes, and letters to the editor to call-in talk shows, rap lyrics, and pamphlets to fanzines, newsletters, articles, and books. Such applied theory might come from a nurse practitioner complaining about unhealthy hospital conditions, or a radio disc jockey condemning government censorship rules, or a minister rebutting a church doctrine. It can derive from outsiders as well as insiders. While there is no difference in kind between academic and vernacular critical theory, the former, according to McLaughlin, is generally more scholarly, rigorous, self-reflective, and formal. "The most important role of vernacular theory in everyday culture," he argues, "is that it fosters more effective practice and more acute interpretation" (p. 163).

While a broad range of special protocols facilitates different vernacular practices of interpretation, street smarts constitute something of a bedrock. By street smarts McLaughlin means, in a first definition, a set of common rules of thumb that he learned growing up in postwar working-class Philadelphia neighborhoods and suburbs. People there knew and acted consciously and unconsciously upon such maxims:

> Everyone knew that politicians lied because they were in someone's pocket, that doctors and lawyers used their position for profit, that priests and nuns were high-minded but not to be taken seriously as guides to everyday life, that bosses were not to be trusted when they

said they had your interests at heart, that teachers and principals were more interested in rules and order than in the needs of kids. There was still a degree of respect for people in power, since it was thought they got their power with their brains, but there was no awe.... [I]t was possible to resist by mental cunning and a strong sense of self-worth. (pp. 28–9)

Armed with street smarts, readers are able to question things and imagine alternatives. McLaughlin is careful to locate the above protocols of interpretation in a particular time and place, being quietly attentive to class, race, religion, and nationality. If one happened to be a young black woman in apartheid-era urban South Africa, other street smarts would no doubt have been in operation. Interestingly, such communal beliefs do not lead to uniform interpretations. Readers, notes McLaughlin nodding assent to the standard pluralist argument, "perceive and interpret texts in idiosyncratic ways, depending on their education, their assumptions about reading, their social identity, and their personal history" (p. 43).

There are, as McLaughlin points out, literally tens of thousands of fanzines in print and online. These are characteristically amateur magazines produced by fans of a film or band, speaking often critically from their expert knowledge. Even the best guides to zines only scratch the surface. They come and go with wild irregularity and rapidity. McLaughlin samples mainly popular music ones in his case study, observing "Zines establish vernacular interpretive communities" (p. 66). Thereafter, he proceeds to discuss several dozen interpretive protocols, the street smarts, the applied theory, of the music zine subculture.

Everybody in this universe of readers assumes, to start with, that corporate record labels seek profits above all; that ironic as well as straightforward music enjoyments are acceptable; that creative rewriting and fantasy are fine and good; and that bodily response to music and musicians' physical energy count for more than their technical polish or artistic skill. Moreover, popular music zine fans position themselves as outsiders, often rebels, sharing unorthodox lifestyles and speaking independently with high attitude (disdainful resistance). When it comes

41

to disputes within fandom, subtle formal distinctions of style and genre, plus the expert application of biographical and historical data, drive interpretive debate. Three additional central protocols of interpretation function within communities. First, a vernacular interpreter is obliged to trace the roots of a band with the goal of assessing its degree of originality and creativity. Repetition of forerunners is a fault. Second, the fan critic must specify with an insider's precision the genre, sub-genre, and sub-subgenre of a band, which is intimately connected to lifestyle and subculture. For example, "It's not just metal but hardcore, not just hardcore but straightedge" (p. 70). Third, these applied theorists are expected to examine the historical context of the group and each of its musicians for continuities and discontinuities in style, theme, oeuvre, labels. This puts a premium on fans' expertise in music microhistory.

Popular music critics in the sprawling world of fanzines differ from academic critics of literature by their many distinctive preoccupations, for instance, with the body, personal affect, low culture, alternative lifestyle, ironic standpoint, disdainful attitude, arcane sub-subgenres, authenticity, readiness to rewrite given texts, aesthetic demerits as well as merits, and flagrant use of street smarts. Yet vernacular and academic critics share many key practices and values in McLaughlin's findings. Both respect authorial authority, artistic originality, genre and tradi-tion, technical skill, oeuvre development, repetitive close reading and stylistic scrutiny, institutional analysis, and the representational and expressive powers of art. What most links contemporary academic and vernacular applied theorists is a skeptical disposition, a proclivity to question things and generate critical readings. That is McLaughlin's primary contention.

But it is not clear how gender and class play out in the popular music fan community and the zines. Unlike Radway and Jenkins, McLaughlin does not do ethnography or participant observation, preferring more distanced textual analysis and archival research in his case studies. In retrospect and surprisingly, none of these cultural studies researchers deals with race or nationality. And none discusses the quality as opposed to the competency of fan commentary. There seems to be in much cultural studies research an unspoken faith in working-class and lower middle-class communities and subcultures as harmonious formations untroubled by internal strife.

For all its many strengths, the analysis of vernacular reading communities is open to criticism. It sometimes romanticizes ineffective social grumbling and griping. It lends prominence to too many purported rebels with too many causes. It co-opts marginal groups. It tends toward leveling counterhegemonic forces into imaginary underground coalitions. It sentimentalizes certain untrained amateurs and seems to denigrate highly trained professionals. It puts a premium on the present and especially on populist elements of it. Lastly, it risks falling in line with the proliferation and flexibilization, the disorganization, of reading in uncritical keeping with our postmodern post-Fordist globalizing era – a time of deregulation, Darwinian "Do it Yourself," Calvinist self-help, short product cycles, market vanguardism, plus hyped leisure and consumer choice. Vernacular applied theory suits the times for good and for ill.

How do things stand nowadays with academic *critical reading* in relation to the numerous vernacular reading communities? There is, of course, a normative academic critical reading. It regularly shows up not only in comparisons between vernacular and academic reading protocols, but in higher education mission statements, study programs for majors, and course descriptions. Critical reading possesses a long history and plays a key role in higher education. Learning to read critically is used everywhere as justification for literary training, both advanced and introductory, and for general education literature courses. Educators, politicians, university trustees, parents, and students believe in the importance of critical reading. At the same time the recent multiplication of academic interpretive communities and the proliferation of postformalist reading conventions mean that critical reading nowadays amounts to an unstable assemblage of numerous often contending practices. Academic courses in critical reading tend, in fact, to be overviews of contemporary schools and movements, typically critical approaches courses that survey formalism, Marxism, poststructuralism, feminism, postcolonial studies, queer theory, and so on. In this context formalism with its related modernist aesthetics serves as unifying scapegoat quietly admired for forwarding the practice of exacting close reading. Significantly, neither Radway nor Jenkins addresses normative academic critical reading, whereas McLaughlin does, arguing that it needs to be taught and is best done so against the background of preexisting vernacular reading practices students bring to class.

In his provocative article "Uncritical Reading," Michael Warner makes a surprising opening connection that combines pious scriptural reading practices with vernacular ones into a peculiar category, namely "uncritical reading." He then pits this against the central category critical reading. Warner regards the latter rightly as a venerable yet increasingly antiquated cultural formation with roots in, for instance, classical Greek genre theory, medieval theories of objective interpretation, and especially Enlightenment ideas of aesthetic disinterest and textual wholeness. Anxiously, he positions himself near the end of the era of Enlightenment-inspired academic critical reading, which he feels is now out of touch with screen and other new literacies. His main task is to denaturalize critical reading, starting with the questionable premiums it puts on distanciation and reserved judgment that enable modern critical disengagement and repudiation. Among the most questionable premises of academic critical reading are the autonomy and individuality of the purportedly free and enlightened reader. In addition, Warner, following historians of the book, underlines the unspoken necessity of the codex with page numbers (versus scrolls), as prerequisite to ubiquitous scholarly tactics of discontinuous reading. Such practices of discontinuous reading range from collating scattered passages into patterns and tracking contradictions to rereading to index-making. These procedures at first glance only appear to involve an ideal of continuous reading and wholeness. Critical reading, moreover, presupposes time, industry, learning, privacy, note-taking, and homogeneous page formats very unlike today's collaged and unnumbered, internet and zine page designs.[9]

Surprisingly, Warner has very little to say about so-called uncritical reading beyond his opening paragraphs that set up his main task, the critique of critical reading. But firmly associated with the students in his literature classes, uncritical readers in Warner's cameo employ nonacademic protocols of reading. For example, they identify with fictional characters, worship authors, seek information and edification, skim and jump around, laugh and cry. "Within the culture of critical reading," observes Warner, "it can seem that all the forms of uncritical reading – identification, self-forgetfulness, reverie, sentimentality, enthusiasm, literalism, aversion, distraction – are unsystematic.... Uncritical modes of reading, it would seem, are by definition neither reflective nor analytic."[10] Warner has much sympathy for his uncritical student readers. He evidently feels that teaching them critical reading is nowadays a rarefied and old-fashioned project. Yet while he appears ready to scrap the required program of critical reading, he does not indicate alternatives. In his three dozen ample footnotes, Warner never cites any of the cultural studies research on vernacular reading. Despite some hedging, he appears to extend little actual credibility to the critical abilities of his student vernacular readers.

Nevertheless, there are three key implications of Michael Warner's provocative, if occasionally too sketchy, article: (1) that scholarly critical reading is one among many modes of reading; (2) that other modes, including uncritical, religious, vernacular, and perhaps pornographic reading, ought to be recognized; and (3) that required courses in critical reading should be supplemented, perhaps scrapped or, at the very least, fully interrogated. Yet insofar as Warner uses tried and true protocols of critical reading to question critical reading, he illustrates their continued usefulness and perhaps inescapability. He does not address the important problem of the cultural capital attached to different modes of reading. And similar to Radway and Jenkins, Warner is not concerned about faults of uncritical reading. Finally, he runs into trouble with the overly dramatic yet memorable catch phrase "uncritical reading," which suggests that students are dupes. The more common neutral term vernacular reading would work much better.[11]

The Enlightenment era gave us modern critical reading. The postmodernity now displacing it is giving us mass literacies and vernacular, uncritical, and heightened pious modes of reading, a pluralization of interpretative protocols and a disorganization of practices both inside and outside the academy. This is the realm of postmodern applied theory. Occupying multiple subject positions, today's reader is advised to assemble and apply varying tactics as situations require. Criteria vary and are flexible. Scholarly critical reading no longer presides uncontested atop a hierarchy of reading practices. It seems, in retrospect, a necessary fiction of a modernist sort. The hegemony of disinterested, objective, secular, and totalizing reading is evidently coming to an end. Displaced by business, religion, and especially popular culture with its many forms and genres, canonical literary discourse and academic critical reading continue to recede in relevance and prominence. While the direction outlined here – the explicit postmodernization of reading practices – is not mentioned by Radway, Jenkins, McLaughlin, or Warner, it is substantiated by their work.[12]

It goes without saying that "close reading" retains high prestige among academic reading practices. Whether deriving from philology, stylistics, formalism, structuralism, deconstruction, or some combination, the strategy of slow, scrupulous, and creative explication of textual details constitutes for many literary intellectuals, especially of older generations, both an indispensable basic skill and the highest attainment of mastery.[13] Being an unconscious value, it goes without saying. No surprise, therefore, that it is not addressed by Radway, Jenkins, McLaughlin, or Warner. But no one that I know wants to get rid of close reading or even to discuss the possibility.

Problems and debates do arise, however, when close reading is still defined formalistically and unilaterally as in the 1950s. In that moment it required not only focus on the words upon the page but also numerous programmatic exclusions: of author's intentions, historical and political contexts, reader's personal feelings, social forces, philosophical concepts, institutional factors, and didactic values. That jettisons everything today's cultural critique wants to examine and New Criticism once tabooed. Such rigidly formalistic close reading is uncritical in the bad sense. It succumbs to dogmatic aestheticism and a purge mentality. During recent postformalist decades, protocols for close reading have become increasingly unprogrammed and more numerous, debatable, and pragmatic. Instruction in close reading for these times consists in teaching slow painstaking line-by-line, word-by-word analysis of texts (manuscripts in some cases) or, more accurately, isolated passages of discourse, attending to all manner of topics, form and style included, with no set list of taboos on what can be investigated. Call it postmodern close reading. The two prime directives of close reading for students remain, however, to uncover subtle and hidden connections, surprising and revealing materials, and to put on display imagination and insight, a talent for discovery. Cultural studies research shows vernacular readers employ strategies of close reading, typically for purposes of criticism and evaluation, especially in making a case against a work. While it has been recently expanded and modified, close reading remains a cherished instrument, however flexibilized, retrofitted, postmodernized.

In concluding this chapter, I insist on bringing in the related issue of modern ideology critique. Surprisingly, none of the four authors discussed here addresses it directly. Should the practice of ideology critique or its expanded postmodernized version of cultural critique hold pride of place in the future, the way it has during the recent ascendancy of cultural studies? While cultural critique has incorporated all manner of interpretive protocols into an expanded academic critical reading, it reserves a central role for Enlightenment ideology critique. To put this question in other terms, Should academic critical reading today focus, whatever else it does, on class tensions and the institutional dynamics and representations of capitalist society and history? While I and the other four authors examined here answer yes, as befits scholar-teachers of cultural studies, we also want to focus on struggles around gender, race, and nationality (not just class), plus accord serious attention to popular culture, including details of its production, distribution, and consumption. We believe in the value of symptomatic reading. None of us is quite comfortable that such broadened cultural critique has recently become orthodox critical reading in many places and characterized as indoctrination. Yet with

47

the evident exception of Warner, no one seems ready to jettison or displace it. This discomfort with the ersatz label of orthodoxy stems from postmodern as well as modern intellectuals' restless capitalist-influenced preoccupation with innovation, vanguardism, cutting edges, and the unorthodox. My own commitment is, when all is said and done, to keep ideology and cultural critique plus close reading as key parts of higher education's expanded training in modes of vernacular and academic critical reading. When it comes to applied theory, this seems to me the minimum educational program today. There is little to be gained in carrying out this mission with a sense of nostalgia, a feeling of ennui, or, worse yet, a guilty conscience. Quite the contrary.

4

Theory Fusions

Interview

This interview took place in April 2005 and was conducted by Nicholas Ruiz, editor of the online journal *InterCulture*. It has been updated and revised.

Nicholas Ruiz: Is theory academically "institutionalized" and, therefore, somewhat of a "docile body"?

Vincent B. Leitch: Yes, theory is institutionalized in some ways, but in some ways not. On the latter point, there is no department of theory, nor a separate discipline. It piggybacks on existing disciplines and interdisciplines, creating fusions. It keeps changing shape, having multiple strands and configurations. Just in the past 15 years or so, there are many more theory subspecialists and very few and increasingly fewer theory specialists or generalists presiding over the whole field. Also it has no specific location now. It's not unusual for someone in geography or architecture, for example, to show up in my class or office. This is theory with a rhizomatous deterritorialized profile.

There are, however, territorializations of theory in institutionalized forms. These include standardized theory courses and curricula, textbooks, guides, reference sources, and websites; specialized journals, special issues of journals, book series, and dedicated shelves in book stores; plus professional organizations (e.g., Society for Critical Exchange, Literary Criticism Division of the Modern

Language Association, International Association for Philosophy and Literature). A handful of recognized US research universities maintain a strong theory faculty and profile. Certain other institutions of theory hold something resembling flagship status: the School of Criticism and Theory's Summer Sessions; the quarterly journal *Critical Inquiry*; the annual Wellek Library Lecture Series in Critical Theory at the University of California in Irvine; possibly the *Norton Anthology of Theory and Criticism*; but certainly the two required survey courses that the anthology caters to, namely the ubiquitous Introduction to Criticism and Theory and Critical Theory from Plato to the Present.

Is theory, thus institutionalized, a docile body? No and yes. No, to begin with, because theory is linked with a set of rambunctious progressive critical forces such as feminism, ethnic and postcolonial studies, queer theory, psychoanalysis, Marxism (including orthodox, Third World, Western, and post–Marxist versions), poststructuralism, and cultural studies. Insofar as theory promotes ideology critique, culture critique, critical thinking, and self-reflection, it is not particularly docile. Its irreverent inquiries into conventions of gender, race, and class alone render it threatening to the conservative hegemonic order, as apparently does its intellectually serious critical attention to popular culture versus canonical culture. Also its long-standing link with aestheticism, that is, anti-utilitarianism, puts it at odds with the status quo.

But the premise that institutionalization engenders or simply means docility is naive. The neoconservative attacks on the university, especially the humanities, which date back in the US to the 1980s Reagan era but continue into the present, suggest otherwise. The quarter-century-long low-grade animosity to tenured radicals in the American university occasionally flares into a crisis or cause célèbre, as in the 2005–6 case of the left-wing Native American professor Ward Churchill. Such incidents remind us there are "dangerous" academics, perhaps under every bush. Academic institutionalization should not be scorned in some knee-jerk way. It has many progressive uses and potentials.

NR: Is theory solely an apparatus for problem identification? Or does it have a broader, even artistic purpose? Is there an aesthetic of problematization?

VBL: Among the primary practical functions of literary and cultural theory today are both *identification* and *problematization*. For purposes of clarification and in my teaching, I often treat these separately. When I read a work of criticism or theory, whether as a referee, reviewer, researcher, or teacher, I inquire into its modes, its identity. That's a major task of criticism and theory. If, for example, I were reading a study of a contemporary American poet, I would ask a repertoire of critical questions concerning its identity. Does it factor in the biography of the writer? In what ways? Is there attention to historical context? What kind of historiography operates here? Are there accounts of modes of distribution and reception of the work? How does tradition figure? Which formal features of literature are scrutinized and which not? Why? What roles, if any, do race, class, gender, age, disability, sexuality, and nationality play? What about language and philosophy of language? Does the critical text have a message? What are its ideological vectors? How does it handle existing knowledge and research? Is it at all critical of its subject? How so? Are there any contradictions? What are its strengths and weaknesses? So here you see that the effort to isolate the distinctive features of a work – to identify it – quickly tips over into uncovering problems.

While I was working on the *Norton Anthology of Theory and Criticism* during the late 1990s, I spun off "Theory Heuristics: Short Guide for Students," a text available at my website, which lays out two dozen ways to both identify and problematize critical works and theories. But there are many more. Doubtless, the street smarts of the vernacular reader, if articulated, would include a substantial number of ways both to identify and problematize discourse.

Parenthetically, there is an Althusserian inflection to the word problematic that deserves mention. It suggests that economic

51

conditions at a certain historical moment – conjuncture – of the mode of production generate problems not to be simply identified and quickly solved. I'm thinking, for instance, of a conflict like that between labor and capital: it depends structurally on the exploitation of the one by the other, as we see today in an innovative (yet old) form such as Wal-Mart, with its million plus ununionized "associates" (almost half of whom are temps without benefits). There are lots of elements that go into this new problematic. What roles, for example, do the law, government, corporations, school, family, and church play in forming and maintaining today's labor conditions? How about gender conventions and the workforce?

To answer your question bluntly, I am reluctant to aestheticize the task of problematization. That said, there is an art and pleasure in putting into operation such productive schema as mentioned above. And, to be sure, there are virtuoso performances of theory and criticism.

I want to make this other point about the broader purposes of theory. The job of problematization does not presuppose a future world free of problems. For a theorist, a problem might be a logical or historical impasse or an unconscious presupposition as well as an outright oversight, a deliberate exclusion, or a purposeful error. In this context, problematization has more of a diagnostic than a straightforward problem-solving mission.

NR: In the midst of theory's consolidating space in the academy, where does the discipline of the humanities find itself today? Is it being subsumed, transformed, or is it obsolescing?

VBL: That's a very broad question, deserving a monograph of its own. I certainly do feel that contemporary theory in our conservative political moment adopts a consolidating posture – a defensive shoring up, (re)dignifying, monumentalizing. But also the dissemination of theory continues apace, it being scattered across many disciplines, specialties, and subspecialties, with no end in sight. Theory fusions are part of its future as well as its past. It's gone capillary and entered the academic DNA. Not surprisingly, there are holdouts, phenomena requiring nuanced inquiries of their own.

How do things stand with the humanities? To begin with, I would break down that large category into its constituent parts, because I believe each discipline deserves separate discussion. I'm thinking of English, classics, history, modern languages, art history, philosophy, etc. In the US context, we usually refer to the standard definition of the humanities established in 1965 in law and current today, which founded the National Endowment for the Humanities (NEH) and was later ratified by the National Humanities Alliance in 1981 (the NHA consists of 80 advocacy organizations and institutes).[1] There are also, of course, humanities wings to some of the social sciences, particularly anthropology, comparative religion, political theory, sociology, international relations. In addition, many of the new postmodern interdisciplines come, in whole or in part, under the designation humanities, such as ethnic studies, gender studies, film studies, semiotics, cultural studies, plus fields like American and other area studies.

If we conceive humanities in this broad sense, and if we factor in all relevant institutional matrices, it is difficult to conceive of the wholesale subsumption or obsolescence of the humanities. Durable institutions of humanities that come immediately to my mind include not only scholarly disciplines, departments, related professional organizations, and humanities centers, but also libraries, publishers, museums, learned societies, foundations, public agencies, public TV and radio. Speaking symbolically and in a US context, the NEH and National Endowment for the Arts (NEA) have survived four decades. They are today comparatively well-funded institutions by admittedly skimpy American standards. Whenever there are periodic calls to close down these two national endowments, usually for moral, financial, or ideological reasons, a broad multifaceted defense is made. There are strong humanities advocates and lobbyists, with the NHA at the forefront, constituting a weighty united front.

It strikes me that today the keyword humanities, however, functions more and more as an administrative category of the university in relation to the three other major academic spheres contending for a share of budgets and a place in the sun, namely the sciences, social sciences, and professions (medicine, law, business, education, etc.). Personally, I rarely think of this term and its improbable constellation in my day-to-day work. It's mainly used by administrators and external critics of the university. When a vice president or legislator invokes the term humanities, it's usually in the context of budget struggles. In this sense the word holds negative connotations for me. I realize it's a different situation in other nations and in small colleges and community colleges, where divisional structures often take priority over departmental units.

Derived historically from the ancient trivium/quadrivium, seven liberal arts, and Renaissance and Enlightenment humanisms, the term humanities also today summons up nostalgia for earlier happier days when the other three areas held less prestige and captured less financial and human resources.[2] This entails a well-known conservative narrative of decline. To illustrate, my father studied Greek and Latin in the 1930s. I studied Latin, French, and German during the 1960s. My children studied French, German, and Japanese in the 1990s. The Greek and Latin classics no longer hold center place in liberal arts curricula. The Great Books are apparently giving way to minority literatures and popular culture, especially TV, music, film, and digital media. Humanistic values are losing ground against scientific and practical ones. This standard negative account pits two systems of value against one another: (a) general knowledge, advanced literacy, refined and balanced judgment, intellectual discipline, critical thinking, appreciation of the arts, and historical and ethical awareness, versus (b) triumphant specialization, efficient quantitative assessment, technical skills, risk–benefit calculation, the arts for display of wealth, studying foreign language for business use and philosophy for efficient argumentation. This is a typical morose narrative of the subsumption and obsolescence of the humanities. But if we set that against the NHA and the alive-and-well NEH and NEA, embattled but fighting on, it's a mixed story for the humanities today at least in the US.

All that said, I believe we humanists must band together and continue to fight over budgets, space, public relations. We must battle against censorship, insidious quantification, the misuse of history, amoral technoscience, antisocial economic and business policies, and the wholesale corporatization of the university. And we must use offensive as well as defensive tactics, all in the name of the humanities, acting as a united front for mutual benefit and the public good.[3] Still, in my experience these battles are special occasions, usually crises. Strong academic unions would be a better solution for many of our problems just now.

You know very few academic people call campus humanities institutes or centers home. Visits there tend to be infrequent, like a holiday or vacation. The specialized department remains the central structure of the research university and liberal arts college in the US and elsewhere, not at all peripheral like the synthetic category humanities is in most instances. Community colleges are another and different matter, requiring a separate account. I am aware of no strong department of humanities per se in the system of 200 major US research universities.

Consider. I taught in the Department of Humanities at the University of Florida as my first job in the 1970s. It was staffed with several dozen full-time faculty, drawn from literature, history, philosophy, art, religion, music. It was a teaching not research department. Its primary mission was staffing a required sequence of introductory lower-division undergraduate courses (Western Humanities I, II, III), spanning from the ancient Greeks to the late modern abstract expressionists, existentialists, and confessional poets. But it was put out of business in that decade, following four decades of life. You will not be surprised to learn that the University of Florida's separate research-oriented departments of English, foreign languages, history, philosophy, etc. were enhanced during that period of general growth. We are speaking here of the very moment when

55

the contemporary theory renaissance took off. This latter story I tell in my book *American Literary Criticism from the 1930s to the 1980s* (1988). So in my personal experience theory replaced the humanities, literally.

To sum up, I do believe that the humanities have been transformed in a way that the famous pioneering pre–World War Two American advocates at Columbia University and the University of Chicago would neither recognize nor probably approve.[4] I take that to be the gist of conservative attacks, starting in the 1980s, in particular William J. Bennett's *To Reclaim a Legacy*, Allan Bloom's *The Closing of the American Mind*, and Dinesh D'Souza's *Illiberal Education*. In a certain sense postmodern cultural studies has unceremoniously taken up much of the space of, while displacing and transforming, the modern humanities program. It has done so with its new transdisciplinary reach into the social sciences, notably sociology; its concern with method but particularly theory; its links to vital vernacular materials (especially postwar popular culture versus the Great Books); its wide popularity with scholars and students; and its commitments to standpoint epistemology and social constructivism as opposed to historical and scientific objectivity. Yet, clearly, cultural studies lacks grounding in history, philosophy, foreign language, and the Great Books, all of which very much characterized mid-century modern humanities curricula. Where cultural studies most stands out in comparison, however, is in its theory-driven interests in ideology critique, race-class-gender analysis, non-Western cultures, and evaluations of commodification, market cooptation, and lately globalization. Unlike Cold War humanities, cultural studies and theory countenance social roles for the arts and culture. They do not fear political resistance or explicit counterhegemonic critical thinking. The transformation and updating of the modern humanities, a postmodern humanities, would in my mind look very much like today's fused cultural studies and theory.

NR: How is the currency of interdisciplinarity a product of the consolidation of the past half-century of theory?

VBL: Half century? The fusion and pastiche characteristic of the post–World War Two postmodern period, a result of collapsing boundaries and social implosions, signal, according to Habermas, Baudrillard, Bourdieu, and others, the historical erosion of auto-nomies established during modernity, with the latter spanning from the Enlightenment through modernism. This postmodern erosion affects nowadays, for example, the autonomy of arts, the sovereignty of nation-states, the separation of the public and private spheres, the inviolability of borders. In recent decades, not surprisingly, the autonomy of many academic disciplines has given way, to a greater or lesser extent. It seems an era of inter-disciplinarity. Contemporary theory is born out of this moment. It is an unstable fusion of literary studies, linguistics, psychoanalysis, anthropology, Marxism, philosophy, gender studies, poststructur-alism, new historicisms, cultural studies, postcolonial and ethnic studies, an open-ended postmodern assemblage that in the US context displaces the modernist formalisms dominant from the 1930s to the 1960s.

During the 1970s, the rise of new interdisciplines as well as of theory felt initially like an explosion more than a consolidation. But with the nostalgic antitheoretical culture wars initiated by conservatives starting in the 1980s, theory, that most interdiscip-linary and vanguardist of fields, became in part defensive and interested in consolidation. This period is quickly followed by the spread of cultural studies and posttheory (that is, post-post-structuralism), where we are still today in the US, a moment of broadly disseminated, theoretically inflected interdisciplinary cul-tural studies defensive when political conditions warrant it.

By the way, in the late 1990s I was one of the developers of a Theory and Cultural Studies program at Purdue University, formed in the Department of English, at a time when the philo-sophers in the interdepartmental doctoral program in Literature and Philosophy, which I co-coordinated for a decade, decided against mutating into cultural studies. For them mixing two dis-ciplines in equal measures was okay, but not multiple disciplines in unequal proportions. Then and now there is a limit to interdisciplinarity. Modern autonomy lives on and has its habits and strengths.

Significantly, the departmental structure of the US college and university looks pretty much today the way it did four decades ago. So too does the job market, a great respecter and enforcer of established disciplines. Postmodern interdisciplines like women's and ethnic studies are generally housed in underfunded and nomadic programs or institutes, not departments. So we live in a time of constrained interdisciplinarity. Postmodern implosion thus far has been a partial, a limited phenomenon: nation–states and borders continue to operate; private and public spheres are distinguishable still; the arts remain distinct and recognizable; traditional disciplines retain autonomy and power. Fusions often feel epiphenomenal rather than foundational. *Nota bene*: there does not exist a department of theory anywhere in the US.

NR: What is postmodern interdisciplinarity?

VBL: I argued in a chapter with that title, published in my 2003 book, *Theory Matters*, that university professors are disciplinary subjects (that is, certified specialists); that academic interdisciplinary work, cultural studies included, does not change mainstream disciplines; that the university is a disciplinary institution; and that, nevertheless, the conception of interdisciplinarity is being reconfigured today.

Whereas *modern* interdisciplinarity dreams of the end of the disciplines with their awful jargon and fallacious divisions of knowledge, the newer theory-driven *postmodern* interdisciplinarity respects difference and heterogeneity, proliferating several dozen new interdisciplines such as black studies, women's studies, media studies, cultural studies, postcolonial studies, science studies, disability studies, body studies, queer studies, etc. Significantly, these fields directly challenge modern humanistic objectivity and the idea of the university as a serene ivory tower, rationally organized and disengaged.

They struggle against the hegemonic order, have activist roots, engage in community outreach of a political sort. Still and all, they submit to modern disciplinarity, its requirements, standards, certifications as well as its methods (exercises, exams, rankings, supervision, norms). So it's a mixed phenomenon, postmodern interdisciplinarity.

A key feature of it for me concerns the existence of differences internal to the traditional disciplines. Astronomy has physics, geology, and mathematics, not just as neighbors, but as guests. Literary studies is entangled with history, religion and mythology, psychology, sociology, etc. In recent decades, the autonomy of many disciplines has imploded. Hybridity has trumped purity. But the university, a throwback modern institution, finesses the eruption of difference and the proliferation of new interdisciplines by shoring up traditional departmentalization, occasionally softened by a Humanities Center here and some modestly funded and volunteer-staffed interdisciplinary programs there.

NR: On a lighter note, in the *Norton Anthology of Theory and Criticism* that you published in 2001, all of the theorists selected were born in the 1950s or, by far, exceedingly earlier. Is there an age requirement for theory? Do any theorists working today, born in the sixties or later, strike you as heralding a new era of theory? Or perhaps, is the "natural selection" of the Market, that which increasingly subsumes the University, selecting against theory and theorists?

VBL: When we six editors of the *Norton Anthology of Theory and Criticism* made our choice of figures during the late 1990s, we had a set of criteria for selection. I drew them up as general editor at the start of the project with the consent of our editor in New York. These selection criteria include significance, influence, uniqueness, poignancy, pertinence, and resonance (especially with other figures in the anthology), plus also readability, teachability, length, and translation. Our standpoint was teaching the history of Western theory and criticism from the ancient Greeks to the present

(Gorgias to bell hooks). Out of 300 to 400 potential figures, we selected, in the end, 148. (The anthology is 2,600 pages long.) Of these, two dozen or so were living theorists, a dozen of them baby boomers born between 1946 and 1957. Your question highlights indirectly a dwarfing effect on our contemporaries when they are set in the long duration of theory's history. It's a matter of perspective. There are, of course, theory anthologies that focus solely on the contemporary period. They arguably magnify thin presentist perspectives.

You ask if there is an age requirement of theory. Yes, in a sense. Theory, like creative writing, gets enclosed in the university during the last half of the twentieth century. (This, by the way, tends to cut it off from literary journalists, poet-critics, and public intellectuals.) A Ph.D. or advanced education is the required price of admission nowadays for theorists. That takes time. It's rare for a contemporary theorist to emerge as a major figure before the age of, say, 35 or 40. A wunderkind would be anyone under 30. It's a different universe from music, mathematics, or poetry, where talent and genius can still emerge early.

You ask me to name critics and theorists in the generation born after 1960 who might be candidates for a second edition of the *Norton Anthology of Theory and Criticism*. No deal. In order for a figure to be selected, three of the six editors have to agree. That's a key protocol of our collaborative project. So I won't step out on my own and make predictions. Not incidentally, the collective sifting process in my experience generally turns out better results than shooting from the hip. I should say we are looking toward a new edition in 2010 or so, and I am sure it will include theorists born after the 1960s. Also it may, I hope, go global, including some ancient and modern sources from, for example, Africa, the Arabic world, China, India, Japan, etc., reaching beyond Western traditions.

But you ask an either/or question at the very end there. Either a new era of theory or perhaps Market imperatives against such a possibility. That formulation seems flat wrong to me. The search for the new, like that for the bigger and the better, is precisely in harmony with market imperatives. It is what advertisers, campus boosters included, ceaselessly invoke. I imagine a traditional community would not seek the new, which represents a threat, but rather take comfort and sustenance from the unchanging old.

I believe that the university is being increasingly corporatized, that is, subjected to so-called free-market principles and practices, including a sauve-qui-peut neo-Darwinian philosophy of competition and natural selection.[5] And, of course, this impacts theory (as well as other fields), its institutionalization, its bases in the humanities and "soft" (nonquantitative) social sciences, particularly its current hosts, namely literary and cultural studies programs. Here we are experiencing a whipsaw phenomenon characteristic of the post–welfare state corporate university. On one hand, there is less funding, reduced hiring, more reliance on part-time teachers, increased student–teacher ratios, huge student debt, cutbacks. On the other hand, stepped up competition is occurring in credentials, obtaining grants, getting jobs, securing publication, earning tenure and promotion, staying current. (I discuss this in detail in chapter 6.) So we should expect continued, no doubt increased, obsession with the cutting edge, the new, the hottest thing, young guards, shelf life, etc., especially in state-supported research universities where publish-or-perish criteria are pretty fully joined to neoliberal market values. I figure theory to compete and maintain its allure. But also we should expect fewer regular jobs, more adjuncts, exacerbated class stratification for the professoriate, graduate student debt bondage, proportionally decreased humanities majors.

How will theory fare? It's good news, bad news. Insofar as postwar higher education married the new and theory and insofar as the institution persists in this relationship – as I suppose it will – theory will survive under the aegis and considerable protection of the new, of research, and of market vanguardism. Yet to the considerable extent that "market forces," such as pragmatic administrators, community supporters, and clients devoted to

61

bottom-line utilitarianism, prefer vocationalized education, the humanistic hosts of theory will find their justification and mission tipping ever more toward service functions focused on basic literacies and skills. Private universities in the US will have more latitude here, no doubt. Some leading state universities can be expected to undergo privatization, their state government funding having reached lows near 8 percent of annual operating budgets. All this spells a future of further stratifications in theory research and education.

Part II
Politics

5

Late Derrida

During the 1960s, 1970s, and 1980s, Jacques Derrida, the most influential contemporary theorist, published numerous books, approximately two dozen in French, virtually all translated into English, but in the 1990s and thereafter up to 2004, the year of his death, he brought out roughly three dozen more books in France, not including the revised editions of earlier works, coauthored works, and introductions to books. In this period, which I am here labeling late Derrida, about two dozen books by Derrida appeared in English translation, without counting three substantial Derrida readers. What to make of all this work?

Not surprisingly, recent introductions to Derrida find it especially challenging to systematize such a sprawling corpus. The preferred approach is to foreground key Derridean concepts (so-called undecidables or quasitranscendentals) such as the early theory standbys differance, iterability, margin, supplement, text, and later ones like democracy to come, forgiveness, gift, hospitality, justice, messianic, responsibility, spectrality. This, for example, is how Geoffrey Bennington organizes his well-known "Derridabase" in *Jacques Derrida*, coauthored with Derrida and published in French in 1991, in English in 1993, and revised in 1999 with updated, supplemented bibliography.

A second popular approach to Derrida is the exegesis of key controversies in contemporary theory such as Derridean deconstruction versus structuralism (Saussure and Lévi-Strauss), phenomenology (Husserl and Gadamer), psychoanalysis (Freud and Lacan), speech-act theory (Austin and Searle), communications theory (Habermas), and orthodox Marxism. There are also Derrida's conflictual one-on-one encounters, sometimes numerous and recurring, with major figures of theory like Plato, Rousseau, Kant, Hegel, Nietzsche, Heidegger, Blanchot, Levinas, Foucault, and de Man. The French philosopher Marc Goldschmitt employs this method in his *Jacques Derrida, une introduction* (2003), as does the substantial concluding chapter of *Understanding Derrida* (2004), edited by Jack Reynolds and Jonathan Roffe, an introductory book containing 11 chapters by different hands on standard topics such as language, literature, art, ethics, religion, and politics.

A third way of managing while introducing Derrida's immense body of work mixes and matches key concepts, controversies, and critical encounters, also offering the usual detailed subdivided bibliographies of his works as well as works on him. This, for example, is how Nicholas Royle's student-friendly *Jacques Derrida* (2003) proceeds.[1]

Yet, given the scope and complexity of his corpus, Derrida's scholarly readers and critics, no matter their approach, risk becoming disciples rather than critics, expending copious energy systematizing, deciphering, standing by attentively, ventriloquizing. In this chapter I aim to avoid such pitfalls in my own survey and critique of Derrida's influential late works on politics.

Why the focus on politics? It wasn't until the late 1980s that Derridean-influenced poststructuralism went political. This was the last major wing of contemporary theory to make the change, in the US at least. It did so under pressure from several directions. In 1987 pro-Nazi charges surfaced publicly against Martin Heidegger (Derrida's tutelary figure) and Paul de Man (Derrida's colleague and friend). At the same time poststructuralism was responding to increasingly hostile charges from conservatives waging culture wars. Allan Bloom's *The Closing of the American Mind* (1987) was particularly nasty. Like many other groups of humanists, poststructuralists were also feeling threatened by the university's increasing loss of autonomy at the behest of speeded up corporatization. Moreover, poststructuralism was reacting to pressure stemming from the collapse of the Soviet

Union and the rise of the triumphant neoliberal American New World Order. Derrida's late works respond to these times. This chapter illustrates that claim. The "going political" of one of the main figures and branches of theory – under pressure to do so – very much shapes what living with theory involves nowadays in the early part of the twenty-first century. Notwithstanding some recent quixotic turns to reborn formalism and pure aesthetics, nearly all academic theorists of literature and culture have been firmly disabused of the idea, or even hope, of being above politics.

The many books by and about Derrida during the 1990s set the context for a visit I made to Paris in 2004, a few months before Derrida's passing in early autumn. At that time I encountered several not yet translated texts by Derrida, namely *De quoi demain . . . Dialogue* (For What Tomorrow . . . A Dialogue) (2001), a wide-ranging and lively dialogue with French historian Elisabeth Roudinesco, covering nine representative topics in nine chapters, ranging from the death penalty and anti-Semitism to the changing family and animal rights to psychoanalysis, contemporary philosophy, Marxism, and theories of identity and liberty. There was also *Voyous* (Rogues) (2003), two lengthy speeches that squarely address contemporary politics, taking up such issues as rogue states, international law, democracy, reason, and especially sovereignty. And there was *Genèses, genealogies, genres et le génie* (Geneses, Genealogies, Genres, and Genius) (2003), an appreciation of the work of Hélène Cixous, one of Derrida's favorite living writers and evidence of his lifelong engagement with literature. The political concerns of the first two books also appear, but in a remarkably condensed form, in the contemporaneous English-language casebook *Philosophy in a Time of Terror: Dialogues with Jürgen Habermas and Jacques Derrida* (2003). This work contains a revealing interview about politics with Derrida (as well as Habermas) by the Italian-American philosopher Giovanna Borradori.

The texts published in the opening years of the new century followed an immensely productive prior decade that included a spate of books gathering Derrida's many interviews, specifically his *Points . . . Interviews, 1974–1994* (1992; trans. 1995), *Sur parole: Instantanés philosophiques* (On My Word: Philosophical Snapshots) (1999), and *Negotiations: Interventions and Interviews, 1971–2001* (2002); his dialogues with Italian philosopher Maurizio Ferraris, *A Taste for the Secret* (1997; trans. 2001) and French philosopher Catherine Malabou, *La Contre-allée* (Counterpath) (1999); his many pieces on state education and pedagogy in *Who's Afraid of Philosophy?* (1990; trans. 2002), *Eyes of the University* (1990; trans. 2004), and "The University without Condition" (2001), a short book in French also available in Derrida's English-language collection of addresses *Without Alibi* (2002). In the realms of politics and ethics there were such fin-de-siècle texts as *The Other Heading* (1991; trans. 1992), *Specters of Marx* (1993; trans. 1994), *Politics of Friendship* (1994; trans. 1997), *Of Hospitality* (1997; trans. 2000), *On Cosmopolitanism and Forgiveness* (2001) (two late 1990s addresses joined in this English-only book), and *Marx & Sons* (2002), a small book in French published earlier in English as a lengthy concluding essay addressed to his leftist critics in *Ghostly Demarcations: A Symposium on Jacques Derrida's* Specters of Marx (1999). There is much material to consider.

At a revealing point in the conversation with the philosopher Ferraris, Derrida looked back over his career and observed, "Each time I write a text, it is 'on occasion,' occasional, for some occasion. I have never planned to write a text; everything I've done, even the most composite of my books, were 'occasioned' by a question. My concern with the date and the signature confirms it."[2] Indeed, many of Derrida's texts give the appearance of being thrown together like preliminary thinking exercises, lacking editing, especially for economy and careful organization, performances that amble sometimes loosely, sometimes stunningly. About writing systematic treatises in Kantian fashion, Derrida declared in conversation with Gianni Vattimo, "it is no longer possible to write a great philosophical 'machine'.... I always operate through small oblique essays" (*A Taste for the Secret*, p. 81). Concerning this generic obliqueness, the critic Bennington notes kindly that "deconstruction happens more in the journey than the arrival" and Royle observes that "all of Derrida's work is concerned with the appearance or apparitional effects of digression."[3]

Yet concepts do regularly recur from one Derrida text to another and at times cluster in nodal points and theoretical condensations. They bring into view Derrida's infrastructure, his pharmacy, an ensemble of quasitranscendental concepts, as in the case of sovereignty in the late works, a key political theme neither examined nor assessed with care elsewhere in the scholarly literature on late Derrida. So let me focus on sovereignty as a way to depict and to assess the politics of Jacques Derrida as well as the explicit political turn of poststructuralism in the fin–de–siècle.

Derrida's Deconstruction of Sovereignty

In *Voyous*, Derrida explores several main topics, particularly rogue states, reason, and sovereignty in relation to democracy. Titled "The Reason of the Strongest (Are There Rogue States?)" the first lengthy address, notes Derrida scrupulously and characteristically, was delivered on the occasion of a conference, The Democracy to Come, in July 2002 at Cerisy-la-Salle, while the second, shorter lecture called "The 'World' of the Enlightenment to Come (Exception, Calculation, and Sovereignty)" took place at the University of Nice in August 2002 at the 29th Congress of the Association of French Language Societies of Philosophy. This much is clear about the book's title and topic from Derrida's preface: the rogue state "does not respect its state duties before the law of the world community and the obligations of international law, the state scoffs at the law – and mocks the condition of law."[4] A footnote to this definition immediately questions: "Does the reason of state always submit to the condition of law? Does sovereignty itself relieve it of the condition of law? Or else does it exceed and betray it, always as an exception, at the very moment it claims precisely to establish it?" (*Voyous*, p. 12). Derrida puts the concept of sovereignty in question right at the outset, and the rogue state has everything to do with it. What happens in contemporary politics plays a leading role here, as Derrida illustrates in this and a dozen other late texts.[5]

69

Citing Noam Chomsky's *Rogue States: The Rule of Force in World Affairs* (2000), Robert Litwak's *Rogue States and US Foreign Policy* (2000), and William Blum's *Rogue State* (2001), Derrida confirms "the most perverse, violent, and destructive of *rogue states* would thus be, first, the United States and occasionally its allies" (p. 139). Insofar as this nuclear state stands arrogantly above and disregards international laws and treaties, often in the name of a supremacist nation-state sovereignty, this hegemon simultaneously relies on yet undermines the concept of sovereignty. Can there be several hundred fully sovereign nations in the world? Are limitations necessary? How do things stand with the politics of national sovereignty?

Usually defined as supreme authority within a territory, linked with a historical sequence of sovereigns (god, king, people, nation, will), sovereignty among nation-states dates from the time of the Peace of Westphalia (1648), when interference in other states' governing prerogatives became unacceptable. Following Carl Schmitt, Derrida points out "a sovereign is defined by his capacity to decide the exception," and he has "the right to suspend the law."[6] During modern democratic times this ontotheological right passes to the governing body or leader. In the US, for instance, it manifests itself in the right of the president to grant pardons from judicial judgments. Moreover, a state's "monopoly on violence is of a piece with the motif of sovereignty. It is also what will always have grounded the death penalty, the right of the state, the right of the sovereign to punish by death."[7] In addition to the death penalty, sovereignty enables a state to control its borders and exclude noncitizens as well as to protect itself from outside threats (today that includes forces of globalization and terrorism). In its practice, sovereignty remains connected with the use of force and the principle "might is right."

There are paradoxical nondemocratic features of sovereignty, as Derrida's various deconstructions very strikingly demonstrate. Consider the contradictory idea of *a* sovereign (one over many); the concept of exception (being above the law); the notion of the death penalty (contravening the right to life of the citizen); or the fact that "only small states ever see their sovereignty contested and disputed by powerful states. . . . Powerful states never allow their own sovereignty to be challenged."[8] Additionally, the US in special nondemocratic, contradictory ways not only "plays a virtually sovereign role among sovereign states,"[9] but dominates the elite inner circle of the United Nations (the nondemocratic Security Council), exercising there a sovereign unilateralism:

> As always, these two principles, democracy and sovereignty, are at once and by turns indissociable and in contradiction with each other. For democracy to be real, in order to grant space to a right to assert its idea, and to become actual, it requires the *cratie* [power] of the *demos* [people] – in this case of the global *demos*. Thus, it requires a sovereignty, namely a force stronger than all others in the world. But if the constitution of this force is indeed destined in principle to represent and protect this global democracy, it in fact betrays and threatens it at the outset. (*Voyous*, p. 143; my brackets)

Despite all the contradictions of sovereignty in its modern democratic form, Derrida aimed to preserve it, but in limited and shared forms. Such deconstructive questioning and sharing is what, he pointed out, is in any case happening in today's politics.

The Derridean deconstruction of sovereignty is at once simple and complex. Part of the complexity has to do with sovereignty's bearing on ethics, law, and human relations. Here is Derrida assuming the role of political prophet in the context of the "war on terror":

> This movement of "deconstruction" did not wait for us to begin speaking about "deconstruction"; it has been under way for a long time, and it will continue for a long time. It will not take the form of a suppression of the sovereign state at one particular moment in time but will pass through a long series of still unforeseeable convulsions and transformations, through as yet unheard-of forms of shared and limited sovereignty. The idea and even the practice of shared sovereignty, that is, of a limitation of sovereignty, has been accepted for a long time now. And yet such a divisible or shared sovereignty already contradicts the pure concept of sovereignty. . . . The deconstruction of

71

sovereignty has thus already begun, and it will have no end, for we neither can nor should renounce purely and simply the values of autonomy or freedom, or those of power or force, which are inseparable from the very idea of law. How are we to reconcile unconditional *auto-nomy* (the foundation of any pure ethics, of the sovereignty of the subject, of the ideal of emancipation and of freedom, and so on) and the *hetero-nomy* that . . . imposes itself upon all unconditional hospitality worthy of this name . . . ? (*Philosophy in a Time of Terror*, pp. 131–2)

In Derrida's typically nuanced account, the limiting and sharing of political sovereignty, however contradictory to its very concept, is going on (and will continue to do so), which is a good though risky thing. It is not just the modern system of nation-states and its international components that depend on sovereignty, but also ethics, law, and so on. (More in a moment about this brow-raising "and so on.")

In its very operation, sovereignty functions through and with autonomy, freedom, force (they are essential). Each sovereign exhibits such traits, including importantly the modern citizen-subject. "Human rights pose and presuppose the human being as sovereign (equal, free, self-determined)" (*Voyous*, p. 128). Furthermore, "all the fundamental axiomatics of responsibility or decision (ethical, juridical, political) are grounded on the sovereignty of the subject, that is, the intentional auto-determination of the conscious self (which is free, autonomous, active, etc.)" (*Without Alibi*, p. xix). Thus, concludes Derrida, one cannot simply jettison the sovereign self, its liberty, equality, responsibility, and power, any more than the sovereign nation-state.

Many others have reached the same unsurprising conclusion, though Derrida omits mentioning the copious scholarship on the topic. He develops his position on the sovereign subject while realizing full well that the self of the citizen is, in fact, divided and multiple. Among innumerable statements on this topic, particularly concerning the unconscious and the other (as well as the other in me), here is a very telling one: "instead of a subject conscious of itself, responding sovereignly by itself before the law, we can put in place the idea of a differentiated, divided 'subject,' not to be reduced to a conscious, egological intentionality. And a 'subject' established progressively, laboriously, nevertheless imperfectly, having conditions stabilized – that is, not natural, forever and essentially unstable – for its autonomy: on the ground, inexhaustible and invincible, of a heteronomy" (*De quoi demain*, p. 286).[10] Significantly, Derridean deconstruction has it both ways here ("yes, but" to the sovereign subject), as it does with the sovereign nation–state – and elsewhere with the idea of sovereign asylum cities and sovereign universities.[11] The concept of sovereignty reaches into many areas, starting with god and reason as sovereign. The significance of "and so on" is that the deconstruction of sovereignty – the double gesture of its erosion yet critical maintenance – is underway, and its scope remains unknown. Not only does the principle of sovereignty pop up in unexpected areas, but it invariably finds itself in a struggle of contending sovereignties (as those who work in universities know all too well). In Derrida's late texts, sovereignty extends to god, ruler, reason, nation–state, people, subject, the asylum city, university, and domicile.

In the citation above from *Philosophy in a Time of Terror*, Derrida abruptly juxtaposes unconditional and conditional hospitality in his discussion of sovereignty. Conditional or ordinary hospitality, by definition, offers welcome on condition that the other respects my rules and my way of life. Unconditional or pure hospitality opens itself fully to the unexpected and the unassimilable, wholly other. "These two hospitalities are at once heterogeneous and indissociable" (*Philosophy in a Time of Terror*, p. 129). The one is the condition, is transcendent to the other, and the other is inconceivable without the one. In practice, conditional hospitality limits welcome while retaining control "over the limits of my 'home,' my sovereignty, my 'I can'" (p. 128).[12] Like the self, the domicile is sovereign.

In the closing pages of *Voyous*, Derrida looks back and helpfully observes "Among the figures of unconditionality without sovereignty that have come to me to privilege in recent years would be, for example, that of *unconditional hospitality*" (p. 204). He quickly lists others, including the gift, the pardon, justice, the impossible, reason, the event, and so on. Rodolphe Gasché long ago named similar doubled concepts, with their unconditional (transcendent) and conditional (ordinary) forms, "quasitranscendentals," which, he pointed out, "are situated at the margin of the distinction between the transcendental and the empirical."[13] Unconditionality without sovereignty in Derrida's late work injects hope and idealism, utopian elements, into politics.

Is it perhaps possible to think a sovereign without sovereignty? Yes, answers Derrida. Playing ironically off the title of Heidegger's famous 1960s interview in *Der Spiegel*, Derrida asked rhetorically: "How could you deny that the name 'god to come' just might be suitable for an ultimate form of sovereignty that would reconcile absolute justice with absolute law and thus, like all sovereignty and all law, with absolute force, with an absolute saving power?" (*Philosophy in a Time of Terror*, p. 190 n14). Here it is a matter of belief in the impossible, of messianicity without messianism (to use the terminology of Derrida's *Specters of Marx*), of a democracy to come. The political form of this im-possible messianic democratic sovereign without sovereignty might be, following Derrida: an international court of justice complete with its own autonomous force; or a democracy that takes into account the singularity of each existent beyond the social while respecting the social bond and legal equality; or an autonomous and democratic, unified all-European force;[14] or a New International, an affinity or alliance without nation-state, party, citizenship, or class (and steadfastly critical of these things). What characterizes such vertiginous Derridean utopian politics is destatification and internationalism as well as perfectability and extravagance.

There is a Derridean political pragmatism that operates under the name "negotiation." It regularly develops the well-known deconstructive double strategy/gesture signaled by the recurring formula, sometimes too pat, on the one hand/on the other. About the matter of nation-state sovereignty, for instance, Derrida resolutely declares "according to the situation, I am antisovereignist *or* sovereignist – and I claim the right to be antisovereignist here and sovereignist there" (*De quoi demain*, p. 153). But insofar as Derrida is not an *unconditional* sovereignist, he tips his wily deconstructive hand, throwing sovereignty in question. In any case, sovereignist and antisovereignist are not two separate, dissociated positions. Rather they haunt one another, as should be pointed out of other Derridean quasitranscendental concepts. It is a matter of the conditionality of the unconditional, a key pragmatic feature of Derridean deconstruction.

In the address "On Forgiveness" a surprisingly stark moment occurs when the paradoxical dynamic of Derridean negotiation becomes clear. Here he takes off from the instance of forgiveness, both conditional and unconditional, the latter entailing an ideal noncalculating and gracious forgiving of the guilty as guilty without request or repentance:

> These two poles, *the unconditional and the conditional*, are absolutely heterogeneous, and must remain irreducible to one another. They are nonetheless indissociable: if one wants, and it is necessary, forgiveness to be effective, concrete, historic; if one wants it to *arrive*, to happen by changing things, it is necessary that this purity engage itself in a series of conditions of all kinds (psychosociological, political, etc.). It is between these two poles, *irreconcilable but indissociable*, that decisions and responsibilities are to be taken. (*On Cosmopolitanism and Forgiveness*, p. 44)

In their preface to *On Cosmopolitanism and Forgiveness*, Simon Critchley and Richard Kearney cogently explain Derridean negotiation: "responsible political action and decision making consists in the negotiation between these two irreconcilable yet indissociable demands. On the one hand, pragmatic political or legal action has to be related to a moment of unconditionality or infinite responsibility if it is not going to be reduced to the prudential demands of the moment. . . . But, on the other hand, such unconditionality cannot, must not, Derrida insists, be permitted to programme political action" (pp. xi–xii). On the one hand/on the other. Double bond and double duty. Here I would emphasize: Derridean unconditionals, such as pure hospitality, absolute forgiveness, democracy to come, work on and in the future. Politics explicitly operates there. Still, for me it lacks materialist grip.

There is a further dimension to negotiation and forgiveness in the context of sovereignty. Consider this strikingly blunt statement from Derrida: "since we are speaking of forgiveness, what makes the 'I forgive' you sometimes unbearable or odious, even obscene, is the affirmation of sovereignty" (*On Cosmopolitanism and Forgiveness*, p. 58). The issue is condescension, arrogance, silencing. "Each time forgiveness is effectively exercised, it seems to suppose some sovereign power" (p. 59). Is there, then, a forgiveness without sovereignty? Derrida's dream was precisely a pure "forgiveness without power: *unconditional but without sovereignty*" (p. 59).

The Derridean double bind of political pragmatics often raises the issue of responsibility in decision-making (as above), a difficult topic amplified here and there across the late work. To make a decision when the path is clear, when knowledge points the way, when a rule applies is, according to Derrida, to follow a program and calculation, not in fact to make a decision at all. It entails good conscience, morality, but also irresponsibility. Conversely, responsible decision must bear antinomies and double binds. "The instant of decision must remain heterogeneous to all knowledge as such, to all theoretical or reportive determination, even if it may and must be preceded by all possible science and conscience. The latter are unable to determine the leap of decision without depriving it of what makes it a sovereign and free decision" (*Politics of Friendship*, p. 219).[15] Responsible decision stems from the sovereign subject, who makes an impossible mad leap. Such pure decision starkly opposes the ordinary variety, leaving us in a jam (each time permanently). Whereas earlier Derrida dreamt of forgiveness without sovereignty, here he projects an ideal responsibility dependent on sovereignty. What's it going to be? Sometimes a sovereignist, sometimes an antisovereignist: "Deconstruction begins there. It demands a difficult almost impossible but indispensable dissociation between *unconditionality*... and *sovereignty* (law, power, might). Deconstruction is on the side of unconditionality, even where it appears impossible, and not of sovereignty, even where it appears possible" (*De quoi demain*, p. 153). This can stand as a summary statement on Derrida's vexing deconstruction of sovereignty.

Derridean Politics

All indications are that Jacques Derrida, a secular Algerian Sephardic Jew,[16] was a democratic socialist with libertarian leanings as well as a strong cosmopolitan, someone who expected contemporary globalization, including market economics, technoscience, media, US hegemony, and European integration to alter the world in many ways that compromise the sovereign democratic nation-state for good and ill. Instances of good erosions of sovereignty for late Derrida include humanitarian interventions, the International Criminal Court, the concept of "crimes against humanity," the end of the death penalty (outlawed in the European Union), and the work of certain non-governmental organizations. "We should salute what is heralded today in the reflection on the right of interference or intervention in the name of what is obscurely and sometimes hypocritically called *humanitarian*, thereby limiting the sovereignty of the State in certain conditions."[17] This nuanced praise of sovereignty's erosion is sometimes balanced by Derrida's defenses of the sovereign democratic nation-state, especially in cases where it fends off the global hegemony of one language, of capitalist concentration, of one neoliberal market, of terrorism, of weapons proliferation. "The presence of the state must be limited, but that presence can be vital . . . : to struggle against structures of violent and abusive appropriation, monopolization, and standardization, to defend the rights and potential of (national and international) culture, to liberate space and forces to that end, without, however, programming, inducing, orienting – in any case, as little as possible" (*Negotiations*, p. 67). Under certain conditions, Derrida says yes to the modern sovereign nation-state in its democratic, nonauthoritarian, socialist form. Unfortunately, he was not forthcoming on what democratic socialism might look like.

But in no case could Derridean politics have been communitarian. After examining at length in *Politics of Friendship* the democratic notion of fraternity (liberty, equality, fraternity), Derrida revealed "I was wondering why the word 'community' . . . – why I have never been able to write it, on my own initiative and in my name, as it were" (pp. 304–5). His corrosive critique of fraternity is underwritten by an almost instinctive distrust of community. In the dialogue with Ferraris, Derrida demanded "do not consider me 'one of you,' 'don't count me in,' I want to keep my freedom, always: this, for me, is the condition not only for being singular and other, but also for entering into relation with the singularity and alterity of others" (*A Taste for the Secret*, p. 27). Moreover, to Vattimo he very poignantly declared "place, family, language, culture, are not my own, there are no places that 'belong' . . . My relation to these seemingly communal structures is one of expropriation, of disownership. . . . My point of departure is there where this belonging has broken" (*A Taste for the Secret*, p. 85). During the dialogue with Roudinesco, Derrida connected his discomfit about community to childhood experiences of being identified and typed with hostility as a Jew (pp. 182–5).[18] In "Marx and Sons," he admitted "I am, even today, I must confess – this is, moreover, easy to see – rather insensitive to any 'sense of comradeship.'"[19]

Not surprisingly, Derrida is suspicious of such key political and theoretical categories as social class, party politics, nationalism. Unlike Wallerstein, Laclau and Mouffe, Hardt and Negri, and other leading contemporary left political thinkers, he does not put stock in the new social movements,[20] which in the contemporary period arguably displace party and class as innovative political forces. While I sympathize with Derrida's complaint "need I remind people that I've always been on the left" (*Negotiations*, p. 164), uttered in 1989, I understand people's perplexity. I was and am perplexed. The intensity of broken belonging and the strength accorded the sovereign self cast a long rightward-leaning libertarian shadow over Derrida's left-wing democratic politics. And while I concur with Derrida's self-assessment "I am not an anarchist," I find more telling, though coy, the rider "deconstruction is undoubtedly anarchic" (*Negotiations*, p. 22).

Derrida's most well-known political statement remains, in retrospect, his condemnation of the ten plagues of the post–Cold War neoliberal New World Order in *Specters of Marx* (pp. 81–4). He stood by this sweeping indictment until the end. In summary, these evils, familiar from leftist work, include, first, spreading unemployment, under-employment, and social inactivity, resulting often from calculated deregulation. Second, the massive exclusion from political partici-pation of the homeless and the widespread expulsion of exiles, immi-grants, and stateless persons. Third, the economic warfare between and among the US, Europe, and Japan, which commands disproportionate international resources. (With its admission during the late 1990s into the World Trade Organization, China should now be added.) Fourth, the contradictions between the values of the free market and protectionist barriers and interventionist policies. Fifth, the external debt holding large segments of humanity in thrall, contradictorily excluding them from the market. Sixth, the massive arms trafficking that links scientific research, commerce, and workers' interests such that its suspension would entail major economic dislocations. Seventh, the proliferation of atomic weapons beyond state and market controls. Eighth, the multiplication of ethnic wars guided by irredentist dreams of original homelands and fears of territorial displacements. Ninth, the spread of profit-maximizing virtual states, organized by drug consortia and mafia, that worldwide infiltrate economic and social systems as well as political institutions. Tenth, and most significant in the present context, the unequal application of international law in the interests of certain powerful states devoted to national sovereignty, backed by technical, economic, and military might.

Derrida should have listed other evils of neoliberal globalization, I believe, notably environmental degradation; feminization of poverty; spread of national security apparatuses, secret bases, militarized states, and bombings of civilians; dedication to quick profits, speedups, short-term goals, systematic exploitation; worsening conditions in and spread of racial ghettos and urban slums; and increasing privatization and uneven distribution of basic resources, particularly food, water, energy, land, education, medical care, and credit.[21] Wide-ranging and detailed critiques of *Specters of Marx* famously appear in *Ghostly Demarcations* (1999), where nine critics, among them Ahmad, Eagleton, Jameson, Macherey, and Negri, respond, some sympathetically, some dismis-sively, others carefully and critically. Several criticisms aptly recur in this revealing casebook: Derrida reads Marx too selectively; he jettisons the useful key concepts ideology, social class, base/superstructure, and exploitation; he lapses into philosophically idealist mystical, sometimes religious, thinking; he skirts practical politics, appearing antipolitics; he is voluntaristic and advocates reform, not revolutionary, socialism.

The key theoretical notions of Derrida's inventive political philosophy in the late works are, in my judgment, democracy to come, unconditional justice, pure hospitality, and the messianic without messianism, famously first assembled in *Specters of Marx* and featured regularly thereafter. These Derridean ideals, phantoms, specters, stemming from or shared by the Enlightenment and modernity, haunt the present, orienting critique and doing political work. There is a peak moment in *Specters of Marx* when Derrida summons the coming of a singular other, an event calling for unconditional hospitality, the incalculable and unexpected (although much anticipated and hoped for) impossible messianic democracy to come, figured as a guest, a foreigner, "who or which will not be asked to commit to the domestic contracts of any welcoming power (family, State, nation, territory, native soil or blood, language, culture in general, even humanity), *just* opening which renounces any right to property, and right in general" (p. 65). How does one characterize this vision, this eccentric political projection, a peculiar assemblage of libertarian, liberal, communist, cosmopolitan, and utopian ideas?[22] How do things stand with sovereignty in this scenario? Clearly, the sovereign subject as spectral foreign guest precedes and outweighs the usual sovereignties of home, nation-state, and cultural belonging. That sums up Derridean politics, a suggestive yet troubling mix, on occasion glibly reduced by him to formulas like unconditional/conditional, ideal/practical, on the one hand/on the other, which generate too predictable paradoxes.

This telling tableau from *Specters of Marx* begins with Derrida self-consciously bracketing political pragmatics and negotiation, pitting the "infinite promise" against "the determined, necessary, but also necessarily inadequate forms of what has to be measured against this promise" (p. 65). In more than one place, Derrida in the late work equates the messianic event, justice, and democracy to come with revolution depicted as an interruption, a radical break in the ordinary course of history, a rupture with a system of dominant norms or programs.[23] Derrida believed in "revolution," foreseeing, however, that it must, pragmatically speaking, "come to terms with the impossible, negotiate the non-negotiable that has remained non-negotiable, calculate with the unconditional as such, with the inflexible unconditionality of the unconditional" (*Without Alibi*, p. 277). Yet revolution appears unlikely under such conditions; it seems just so much speculation.

The final tableau I want to evoke in depicting late Derrida's political theory occurs in *Voyous* when Derrida generalizes, quite shockingly at first, "the States waging war on *rogue States* are themselves, in their most legitimate sovereignty, *rogue States* abusing their power. As soon as there is sovereignty, there is abuse of power and *rogue State*. . . . Thus there are only *rogue States*. Potentially or actually. The State is roguish" (pp. 145–6). Because it is in the nature of sovereignty to seek supremacy and use force, the special epithet "rogue state," Derrida argues, is misleading and should be dropped. (No doubt some states are more roguish than others, notably superpowers with supersovereignty who unilaterally break international laws and agreements.) In any case, insofar as the recent "war on terrorism" is not state-based, the era of rogue states appears behind us, despite President George W. Bush's doubtlessly comforting but misleading reactivation of the category. What is most shocking in Derrida's generalization is the severity of his critique of political sovereignty and the nation-state. The category of rogue state becomes useless as well as hypocritical. At this moment faith in the modern form of the state appears paper thin.

Judging Derrida

Having considered more than a dozen volumes of Derrida's late works, not to mention many of the early works, I am most appreciative, particularly with *De quoi demain*, *Negotiations*, *Voyous*, and *Philosophy in a Time of Terror* in mind, of Derrida's theoretical originality and inventiveness, manifested readily in such suggestive, though spectral, quasitranscendental political concepts as hospitality, justice, the messianic, and democracy to come, all created in the course of his deconstructing their ordinary forms. The well-known Derridean critique of traditional binary concepts and the eccentric focus on margins remain today powerful tools for theory. Derrida's commitments to democracy, justice, and internationalism showed him a political optimist, while his ubiquitous nuances and qualifications displayed a seasoned skepticism alert to conscious and unconscious deceptions. It goes without saying that Derrida was a uniquely gifted reader of texts, very often canonical works, an applied theorist capable of finding motifs previously, in retrospect surprisingly, unnoticed. The specters uncovered in Marx's works are astonishing, as is their linkage with Shakespeare's ghost in *Hamlet*. The readings of Kant scattered across the late works, incisive and productive, should be gathered in a Derrida on Kant sampler under such political headings as cosmopolitanism, responsibility, decision, justice, forgiveness, force, reason (i.e., reason of state). Derrida's creative application of psychoanalysis to theory and politics significantly shaped his accounts of otherness, subjectivity, fraternity, and spectrality, justifying with renewed vigor continued psychoanalytical research in an increasingly discouraging environment. I appreciate Derrida's warnings, though often too broad, about the roles of family, comradeship, community, party, and the nation-state in politics. These are useful caveats for the theory and practice of politics. Although suspicious of the concept of hegemony as too homogenizing, he applied it helpfully and judiciously in the late works, usually to characterize expansive US power sometimes in the plural ("hegemonies"). Derrida's adamant secularism should be admired, but I am not so sure about his late dabbling in religion, even though following September 11, 2001, it is difficult for secular theorists like me to continue simply dismissing religion, much as I want to, having endured 12 years of militant Catholic education during two decades of childhood indoctrination. Finally, the way I see things, the end of the Cold War and the rise of the US empire, plus the cultural wars that started during the 1980s, awakened academics to the important role of the public intellectual. It was not the Heidegger or de Man affairs of 1987 that alone did so. Many of the dozens of late works by Derrida respond directly to this epochal transformation.[24] In this light the famous invocation of the emerging New International in *Specters of Marx*, thoroughly counterintuitive, remains heartening, yet too abstract. I'll take the World Social Forum while I await the arrival of Derrida's New International.

There is more to criticize in Derrida's work. The literature in this area is voluminous. Beyond the points I have already made and cited, I would mention several key matters for theory. I include both those missing in Derrida's work such as popular culture, everyday life, capillary power, corporeality, and those theoretical matters avoided like social class, ideology, mode of production. It is a question here primarily of pragmatically oriented historical materialist theory, of ideology and cultural critique. How can one think effectively about longstanding systematic social inequalities in the absence of some such categories and theoretical frames? The very early Derridean notion of "logocentrism" that covers the period from Plato to Lévi-Strauss will not do: it is ahistorical, disembodied, flat. "Late capitalism" works better: it is fully historicized, materially grounded, broadly explanatory. Finally, I am surprised and disappointed by the absence of defenses of the welfare state that one would have expected from Derrida, and that the left so obviously very much needs to mount in these times of triumphant neoliberal capitalism. The welfare state is a significant achievement of human civilization.

In a recent article, Gayatri Spivak concludes that a key task is "to wrench deconstruction from its proper home in 'Comparative Literature,' to let it loose in 'Cultural Studies' so that it can transform its nice nursery of hybrid plantings to reveal the saturnalia of an imagined counter-globalization."[25] Against the US background of an arguably atrophying comparative literature and a thriving, though often shallow and overextended cultural studies, deconstructive theory needs to migrate and transform globalization studies. This scenario, tellingly, addresses deconstruction both as Derridean philosophy and as

83

an interdisciplinary movement characterized by a dissident deportment, (dis)respect for tradition, antinomian and anarchistic sensibility given to internationalist political work and criticism.[26] Of course, Spivak has long been a poster person for this project while remaining critical of its Eurocentrism and its (mis)handling of subalterns. What is encouraging here for Spivak, and for me, is deconstruction's movement in Derrida's late works not only to politics, but to social science — a trajectory followed by cultural studies, although the latter foregrounds sociology more than political science, history, economics, and international relations. Deconstruction's reckoning with sociology is for the future perhaps. Meanwhile, one of the many forms of counterglobalization evoked by Derrida is an archipelago of rogue groups, a roguocracy to use his term, which transgresses nation-state power and poses a counter-sovereignty to the sovereign state.[27] For good and for ill.

6

The Politics of Academic Labor

Disorganization of higher education in the US has been going on since the 1970s, but most visibly during the past decade or two.[1] Tensions have increased within and among new for-profit entities, online ventures, two-year community colleges, traditional four-year and comprehensive institutions, and research universities. Everywhere the proportion of faculty has decreased in relation to staff, administrators, and nonacademic professionals (e.g., information technologists, public relations specialists, student advisors, fundraisers). Salary and resource differentials among the faculties have risen, with medical, legal, business, and engineering faculties pulling significantly ahead of those in, for example, philosophy, fine arts, history, foreign languages, and English (humanities). Meanwhile, administrative pay has ballooned. While the wages for faculty have flattened out in the large middle, currently ranging from roughly $47,000 to $80,000 for most full-time tenure-track humanities professors, differences between high-end endowed chairs and low-end adjunct teachers have helped generate a historically more stratified and tension-filled internal class system. Simultaneously, the professoriate has been reengineered, with more than 50 percent of all contact teaching hours at the start of the new century performed by casualized teachers, that is, tenure-ineligible instructors and lecturers, part-time faculty, short-term post-doctoral staff, and graduate teaching assistants.[2] Moreover, part-time academic labor doubled between the 1960s and 1990s, going from 20 to more than 40 percent of the teaching labor force.[3] Although the job market in many fields collapsed in the early 1970s, doctoral programs have continued to turn out numerous Ph.D.s, fewer than half of whom in many disciplines have found full-time tenure-track jobs, the rest joining the ranks of casual labor or leaving the profession. At the same time, higher education funding has relied increasingly on outside grants, private and corporate giving, profits from intellectual property and ancillary services, plus of course rising student tuitions, the latter ever more dependent on consumer debt (personal loans and credit cards). In retrospect, it is clear that the numerous changes of recent decades amount to a significant transformation of higher education.

Today's postsecondary education sector, of course, reflects the larger downsizing of the welfare state built up from the 1930s to the 1960s and disassembled since the 1970s, notably during recent politically conservative decades. It is no surprise that faculty unions have emerged in the US during this period. The American Association of University Professors (AAUP), American Federation of Teachers, and National Education Association occupy the forefront. By the mid-1990s more than 60 percent of full-time faculty in the public sector were unionized.[4] Private institutions as well as research universities held out. There are some notable exceptions such as the University of California at Santa Cruz, City University of New York, University of Florida, State University of New York system, Rutgers University, Temple University, and Wayne State University, all unionized. Significantly, however, faculty union contracts have rarely covered casual labor, a historical oversight, with the result that contingent faculty and graduate students have been largely left to their own devices. This is disorganization at arguably its worst. Although there was a Teaching Assistants union as early as 1969 at the University of Wisconsin, it wasn't until the 1990s that TA unionization spread. By 2000 there were 26 graduate student unions on 62 US campuses and 20 more in Canada.[5] The numbers have continued to increase.

Teaching Assistants have many grievances. Time to degree, in the humanities, for instance, has doubled since the 1960s, averaging now nine years after the B.A. for literature and language Ph.D.s. People are starting careers in their mid-thirties, often with young families and large debt burdens. By graduation TAs at state universities have taught anywhere from 15 to 35 courses. Not uncommonly, they have delivered many conference papers and published several articles, often with a book manuscript in progress. Contemporary graduate students have had to professionalize themselves much earlier and more thoroughly than previous generations.[6] Moreover, they spend two to five years in the job search, where most will not succeed in securing full-time tenure-track jobs. TAs rarely get a living wage, health insurance, life insurance, childcare benefits, or a role in governance. Even when they get some of these things, they don't get them all. Forget retirement plans. The landmark 1995–6 strike at Yale University where TAs seeking formal union recognition withheld end-of-semester grades, organized by the campus Graduate Employees and Students Organization (GESO), affiliated with the Hotel Employees and Restaurant Employees Unions of Yale's clerical, service, and maintenance workers, symbolizes some of the worst tensions and disorganization of the contemporary higher education system. It pit TAs against undergraduate students and administrators. Many alumni and almost all faculty sided against the TAs.[7] As the blue-collar affiliation of GESO highlighted the proletarianization of the TA corps, it evidently offended administrators and faculty, comporting ill with the antiquated elitist image of Ivy League professionals kindly doling out patronage to aspiring apprentices.[8]

My first real union job was as a "hod carrier" in Local 66 on Long Island in New York. That is a quaint term for common laborer in the construction business. As a university-aged worker, I wrestled jackhammers, poured concrete, and lugged bricks and cinder blocks up scaffolds. The first time I walked into the union headquarters (this was during the 1960s), I was struck by a huge gold banner, declaring in black letters "Unionism is Americanism." I had reason to believe that at the time. Today it strikes me as an undecidable. Of course, more than a third of the US labor force was unionized then whereas

87

now it has dropped to less than half that number. The labor force is in disarray.

When I got lucky and landed my first full-time academic job during the 1970s in a small private liberal arts university in Georgia, following two years of searching, I became an AAUP activist on the local and state levels. I advocated for faculty benefits, rights, and collective bargaining. Although it was impossible legally to unionize a private church-affiliated Southern institution, I allied myself with public system faculty, hoping for spillover effects. In 1976 the Georgia AAUP conference (composed of 20 state and six private higher education institutions) won the AAUP Konheim Award, given annually to a model conference. In this case it was for instituting a bold and successful lawsuit against the State Board of Regents for rescinding over the summer of 1974 $12 million in annual contracted pay raises. I was on the executive committee, serving as treasurer and director of the Conference Legal Defense Fund. It was a proud yet frantic and frustrating time since, as usual, too few faculty participated. The organizing work was all overtime and unremunerated. Not surprisingly, today I advocate TA as well as faculty and part-time unionization, and I recommend regional and national affiliations. In recent times pockets of the union movement have done well. At the same time, I am aware of the shortcomings of unions, ranging from high dues and historical misuse of funds to narrow guild orientations and fixations on pay and benefits to nondemocratic tendencies and defensive postures.

As a literary and cultural theorist, I have been asked increasingly during recent years by graduate students how theory relates to academic labor. That depends in part on how one defines theory. Here is a working definition my five editorial colleagues and I sketched in writing our preface for the *Norton Anthology of Theory and Criticism*: "theory now entails skepticism toward systems, institutions, and norms; a readiness to take critical stands and to engage in resistance; . . . and a habit of linking local and personal practices to the larger economic, political, historical, and ethical forces of culture."[9] The relations among individual academic job seekers, faculty and TA organizations, the higher education industry, and the broader economy and social order call out for analysis and critique as well as transformation through unionization and other remedies. This is particularly so if one espouses theory and cultural studies. The tools, the gear, of the theory trade – for example, ideology and cultural critique, history from below, deconstruction of norms, institutional analysis, race–class–gender inquiry, not to mention classical self-reflection – all mandate investigation of current professional regimes.[10] Coming from a contemporary cultural studies perspective, I, like many others, consider the links of theory, education, and labor to be substantial, longstanding, self-evident and, to be sure, open to teaching as well as critical analysis and political change.

There is a substantial body of literature by theorists concerning the recent plight of US academic labor. Let me mention some pioneering sources. In *Will Teach for Food: Academic Labor in Crisis* (1997), edited by Cary Nelson, eight articles analyze the Yale strike and another eight address the crisis beyond Yale. In his *Employment of English: Theory, Jobs, and the Future of Literary Study* (1998), Michael Bérubé has a chapter criticizing the Yale faculty and another laying out recommendations to ameliorate the job situation for English Ph.D.s. There have been many dozens of relevant articles and reports on academic labor conditions published, for instance, in the Modern Language Association's (MLA) annual *Profession* as well as its two affiliated *Bulletins*, brought out thrice yearly by the Association of Departments of English and the Association of Departments of Foreign Languages. Numerous reports and recommendations from the AAUP, Conference on College Composition and Communication, National Council of Teachers of English, and other North American specialty organizations are relevant here as well. Perhaps most revealing is the 1997 *Final Report of the MLA Committee on Professional Employment*, a substantial collective document with several leading theorists involved, widely read and occasionally criticized. There is also the engagé material appearing in *Workplace: A Journal for Academic Labor*, a pioneering online biannual published since 1998.[11] The journals *Social Text* and *Minnesota Review* regularly run pieces on academic labor.[12] Other journals do so less regularly, although the weekly *Chronicle of Higher*

89

Education is informative. A key website is hosted by the Coalition of Graduate Employee Unions (founded in 1992) which, among other things, reports on its annual conference and which greeted the new century by posting the cogent document *Casual Nation* (December 2000) that depicted the scope of the crisis, providing charts and graphs and advocating unionization across all fields. There are, of course, other pioneering sources and theoretical documents such as the wide-ranging collections *Chalk Lines: The Politics of Work in the Managed University* (2000) and *Steal This University: The Rise of the Corporate University and the Academic Labor Movement* (2003), plus Gary Rhoades's critical study of union contracts, *Managed Professionals: Unionized Faculty and Restructuring Academic Labor* (1998).

The most trenchant theorist of the current academic labor situation is Marc Bousquet, founding editor of *Workplace*, one-time chair of the MLA's Graduate Student Caucus, and currently tenured Associate Professor of English. A representative piece, published in 2002 in *Social Text*, is his "The Waste Product of Graduate Education: Toward a Dictatorship of the Flexible." Bousquet suggestively outlines three contemporary waves of theorizing about US academic work, including (1) 1960s–1970s ideas and strategies surrounding initial faculty drives for unionization; (2) 1970s–1980s free-market doctrines attending casualization; and (3) 1990s–present labor theories coming from graduate student union organizing. As an activist in the latter new social movement, Bousquet works on two main fronts. He criticizes the hegemonic yet obsolete neoliberal job *market* theory of the 1970s, which the MLA and many faculty (leftists included) still propound. Meanwhile, he has developed his own account of what's really going on.

Forget supply and demand explanations of the so-called job market, argues Bousquet. Earners of doctoral degrees are the waste product, the "excrement," of the higher education system for whom degree completion typically signals the end, not the start, of a lengthy teaching career. The system of academic labor needs new graduate students to do most of the teaching, not new Ph.D.s. Degree holders are being replaced by nondegreed labor in harmony with the corporate downsizing of late capitalist times. All of this reflects as well as aids and abets the ongoing disorganization of the academic workplace. Here is Bousquet:

> that labor system exists primarily to recruit, train, supervise, and legitimate the employment of nondegreed rather than degreed teachers. This is not to say that the system doesn't produce and employ holders of the PhD, only that this operation has become secondary to its extraction of teaching labor from nondegreed persons, primarily graduate employees and former graduate employees now working as adjunct labor – as part-timers, full-time lecturers, postdocs, and so on.[13]

With casual labor accounting for more than 50 percent of all teaching contact hours, it is hard to dismiss Bousquet's argument. Casualized workers constitute a reserve army of labor, exploited more or less everywhere in the US. Were the casual workforce capped at, for example, 15 percent of an institution's total instruction, as recommended by the AAUP in 1992,[14] the gross oversupply of Ph.D.s would turn into a shortage. So it is a mystification that there has been in recent decades a decreased demand for Ph.D.s: demand has been met by squeezed labor.

If you happen to be a doctoral student, such theory is, I believe, required reading. If you are faculty, staff, administrator, trustee, regent, or politician, not to mention undergraduate student or parent, it points to questionable stewardship, if not willful blindness or plain indifference. It vividly exposes a "pyramid scheme," to use Cary Nelson's provocative term,[15] underlying the free-market practice of permatemping that today affects large segments of the labor force (not just academe) systematically stripped of benefits and subject to social insecurity.[16]

One of my first glimpses of things to come occurred during the early 1970s in the year I was completing doctoral studies. A notice appeared in the spring issue of *PMLA*, advertising a Postdoctoral Intern-Fellowship Program at a large research university in the

South as a "unique new plan." Indeed, it was. Being unsuccessful on the job market that year, I was a captive audience. The plan offered new Ph.D.s a salary half the normal beginning tenure-track one, a weekly nine-hour teaching load, in-service training and supervision, plus assistance in the job search. I wrote an angry ironic letter appearing in the *MLA Newsletter*. I pointed out most new Ph.D.s had already received training, supervision, and job assistance. The only thing new here was the exceedingly low wages. The program was, in fact, "feeding off the desperation of the unemployed intellectual proletariat." Further, I wondered out loud whether the state university in question had "hired new professors this year. Hiring ten fellows instead of ten assistant professors could save a lot of money." A reply from the Vice President for Academic Affairs accompanied my letter in print. It noted that 648 applicants had applied; that they were "no exaggeration – desperate"; and that "(1) we did not create this desperation; (2) we did not force anybody to apply."[17] I cite this exchange not to pat myself on the back as a visionary. Quite the opposite. More than three decades ago it was evident even to a neophyte that the academic labor force was being altered via casualization.[18]

My letter made it clear I was responding based on interviews with a dozen doctoral students. I was on the Executive Committee of the local Graduate Student Organization. What we perceived at the onset of this transformation of the academic labor force was a "crisis," not a "condition."[19] It took another 20 years or more to figure this out. In hindsight, that seems unbelievable. The intervening years were filled with expectations of better times to come; promises of imminent widespread retirements and replacements;[20] sporadic cutbacks in graduate admissions by a few isolated departments; hopes of returning to late 1950s–early 1960s conditions of job abundance; and a short-lived upturn in the 1980s job market. But by the mid-1990s amidst a seemingly full-blown US economic boom, yet a continuing depression in academe, it was finally clear that the labor crisis in higher education was not going away. A new wave of academic unionization drives began. This occurred even at some research universities where faculty and doctoral students tend to see themselves as individual free agents and entrepreneurs, traditionally identifying with the aristocracy, professional guilds, and administration rather than the national teaching corps or the working classes.

During the seventies as a tenure-track Assistant Professor with a spouse and two young children, I qualified for federal food stamps. I promptly received them, much to the astonishment of my colleagues and dismay of my administration. After all, I was being paid the going academic wage. This was one of several anarchistic job actions carried out in the decade after receiving my Ph.D. When I moved to Purdue University in the mid-1980s, a large Midwestern state research institution, I was stunned by how minuscule faculty and student union sentiments were. But the fact is these were counter-revolutionary years: the AAUP lost half its membership, shrinking from roughly 75,000 to 45,000 members; President Reagan busted the 13,000-member flight controllers' union and got away with it; accelerated deindustrialization everywhere dramatically eroded formerly well-paid workers' security; and a short-lived spike upwards in the academic job market took considerable pressure off. Demoralization and disarray worsened throughout the 1990s as rampant explicit casualization of labor, swelling enrollments, legislative defunding of public institutions, and triumphant free-market corporate management theory and discourse (the jargon of "excellence") assaulted higher education. By then there were no food stamps to be had, the welfare state having been in the meantime dismantled piece by piece, with welfare clients gleefully tossed onto the labor market during the second Clinton term.[21]

From the 1970s onwards, more and more has been written, particularly within cultural studies circles, on postindustrial, post-Fordist, postmodern political economy.[22] An inventory of key words and buzz phrases would turn up a wide array of telling, now all-too-familiar terms: downsizing, deregulation, privatization, flexibilization, debt, free trade, transnational corporation, good business environment, two-earner family, individual retirement account, shareholder revolution, quarterly profits, bottom line, commodification, International Monetary Fund (IMF), World Trade Organization, globalization, plus plenty of others. Yet comparatively little has been written on the new political economy of higher education by senior cultural studies figures, with a few notable exceptions most already mentioned. There is, nevertheless, a burgeoning subfield of cultural studies scholarship – academic labor studies – created by young activists and mid-career sympathizers, all of whom deplore corporate images of professors as content providers, students as customers, and higher education institutions as profit centers and engines.

Like others, I see here a main faultline running through not just US politics, but current globalization politics worldwide. It concerns the dispute about the place and scope of market practice and theory. When it appears, this dispute typically pits outraged progressives and worried centrists against arrogant free-market fundamentalists. Not surprisingly, the struggle against decreasing regular faculty and increasing casual labor reiterates key elements of the battles against, for instance, IMF conditionality agreements (vanguard free-market "agreements"). In both cases, funding generally occurs in an explicit neo-Darwinian environment of ruthlessly reduced spending, low wages, worsening work environments, narrowed tax bases, high wages for management, systematic cuts in social insurance, increased administrative decision-making, and growing insecurity.[23] Triumphant market logic seeps into every corner of life. Free-market discourse is the dominant genre of our time, trumping politics, religion, ethics, health, entertainment, and education. Much autonomy in these spheres has been ceded to market criteria. In healthcare, for example, recent decades have witnessed drastic cutbacks in (as well as temping of) hospital nursing and technical staff; increased case loads and speed-ups; the American Medical Association advocating unionization of doctors; numerous public hospitals sold off; munificent pay for top hospital and health insurance administrators; 47 million people in the US without health insurance; privatization of Medicare drug benefits; the triumph of neoliberal administrative rationality across the system; worsening health care. The situation of academic labor is of a piece with labor elsewhere in the new economy, a point illuminated by cultural studies work on the topic.

94

"Theory" in postmodern times is a banner under which a whole set of progressive social movements have gathered, ranging from feminism to queer theory, Third World and postcolonial liberation to equal justice for ethnic minorities, psychoanalysis to Marxism in their classical and contemporary forms. For academics in many literary, linguistic, foreign language, and other humanistic and social science disciplines, theory is a ticket as well as a banner. Job announcements regularly feature it as a preferred strength. It is more or less an essential element in framing research, including conference papers, articles, dissertations, grant proposals, and job applications. It forms a large part of the technical language and unconscious of the professoriate. It shapes not only research and professional discourse, but classroom teaching, it being expected that theoretical concepts and issues, if not primary texts, will appear in course syllabi. There is much theory work to be done, with, for example, a large and growing library of guides, primers, and readers aimed at every level of student and all types of courses. Theory shows up not just in courses, credentials, and research projects, but teaching portfolios and experiences.

Theory is both banner and ticket, which is how things work in our late capitalist postmodern society, the higher education industry not excluded, having been increasingly flushed from its liberal gated walls and tossed onto the conservative forcefields of competitive niche markets. Under such conditions, it has become less and less possible or conscionable to keep political economy – for instance, exploited labor, downsizing, privatization, and (de)unionization – out of guild publications, conference proceedings, scholarly journals, and the theory curriculum. Everywhere free-market economics reconfigures erstwhile autonomous spheres toward the goal of maximun productivity and fast profits in disregard of decent sustainable living conditions, to say nothing of social justice. This is one conflict theorists must teach. Call it political economy, postmodern culture, late capitalism, neoliberalism, corporatization, globalization, work theory, or what you will.[24]

Many academics in the US are laboring 50 and 60 hours a week (unpaid summers included). This is especially so for beginning tenure-track professionals and casual workers, for whom the credentials ante has been mercilessly upped in the face of the vast reserve army of Ph.D.s. This overemployment wreaks havoc on personal and family life.[25] Meanwhile, the large and growing number of underemployed and unemployed Ph.D.s exceeds estimate. Stress and anxiety affect not just academic laborers but the workforce at large, employed and not. The old goal of a 30-hour work week now seems quixotic. But wouldn't it be great if we could shift 20 hours or so per week from the overemployed to the un- and underemployed? No doubt, it is utopian to think so.

When I arrived at my present university, the University of Oklahoma, we had 30 full-time English Department faculty with a campus enrollment of 21,000 students. As I write this nine years later, there are 28 faculty and 27,000 students. The number of TAs has jumped from 40 to 55 while contingent teachers have held steady at around 15–20. However, several years ago we added a new category of casual worker to our departmental bylaws, "term faculty," with length of employment not to exceed six years. Five are presently on staff. In other words, considerable financial support has been (and continues to be) shifted outside the department. During my previous decade at Purdue, a Big Ten public university, more or less the same scenario obtained. There were 50 full-time English faculty and 33,000 students on my arrival, and 40 faculty and 35,000 students upon my departure. The TA number held roughly constant at 150 while part-timers went from 20 to 40. Needless to say, class sizes increased at both universities, as did numbers of majors and faculty service loads. Some distinguished positions were added, though overall full professor lines decreased. Each campus hired full-time professional advisors for majors, a mixed blessing, freeing up faculty time yet reducing faculty contact with students while adding to the ranks of administration. At both institutions more assistant deans, fundraisers, PR staff, IT specialists, athletic directors, professional security personnel, and well-paid administrators were hired, marginalizing the role of and budget for faculty and instruction. In addition, lots of new buildings, parking lots, stadium enhancements, fountains, spas, landscaping, and cleared parcels of land popped up. Both schools successfully campaigned for $500 million of private gifts, all the while raising tuitions far beyond inflation rates while facing reduced annual state support. At the University of Oklahoma state government contributions to the annual operating budget dropped from 36 percent in 1993 to 20 percent by 2005. During this period student tuition and fees jumped from covering 12 percent to 24 percent of the yearly budget. Nowadays only 30–10 percent or sometimes less of yearly budgets come from state legislatures, and the number keeps declining, speeding up privatization. Based on my experience, this is what in broad strokes the state-supported public research university looks like in the US. I realize that compared to many liberal arts and community colleges plus universities abroad things are not so bad for faculty at American research universities. There are many circles in purgatory.

How do things stand for senior professors, distinguished faculty, endowed chairs, the privileged teaching class? This question is rarely posed, but deserves asking. Consider Stanley Aronowitz's summary on the disorganization of the professoriate which he focuses glancingly on the full professor:

> Academic labor, like most labor, is rapidly being decomposed and recomposed. The full professor, like the spotted owl, is becoming an endangered species in private as well as public universities. When professors retire or die, their lines frequently follow them. Instead, many universities, even in the Ivy League, convert a portion of the full line to adjunct-driven teaching, whether occupied by part-timers or by graduate teaching assistants. At the top, the last good job in America is reserved for a relatively small elite.[26]

The picture here is of a stratified academic workforce where increasing numbers of part-timers and TAs reside at the bottom of the heap, with fewer Assistant, Associate, and Full Professors further up the scale – a scale topped off by distinguished and endowed chairs. This resembles a caste system occupied at its top by Brahmins and its

97

bottom by untouchables. While the academic profession used to resemble a broad middle class having some short-term apprentices and adjuncts, it now consists of a large and growing proletariat, a shrinking middle class, and a tiny yet stratified elite.

(In assessing this chapter, one of the publisher's two referees of *Living with Theory* wondered about its tone. While the book is upbeat on theory, this chapter is noticeably glum on academic working conditions. What is the relationship? The fact that theory has proliferated, especially under the aegis of cultural studies, appears unrelated to the worsening plight of labor. Certain relations, however, do clearly pertain. Consider the US context. As in any grocery store, Wal-Mart, or shopping mall, on display is a growing abundance of items and choices, increasingly produced, shelved, and bought by underpaid and unprotected, insecure workers. That is pretty much the situation of theory in recent times. We see increasingly vulnerable consumers (students) and producers (faculty) amidst abundance. Some higher-ups do very nicely, as the pyramid model illustrates. On the one hand, theory answers late capitalist calls for innovation, flexibility, and productivity. There is no longer any surprise in such inflexible market demands. On the other hand, theory has become ever more critically and publicly engaged as political and economic conditions have visibly worsened. This chapter illustrates that claim. Speaking more broadly, a wide range of theories enter into the picture. Most prominent here are Marxism, feminism, race studies, postcolonialism, and cultural studies. Nowadays they often address politics, labor included, directly. Here, there, and seemingly everywhere the garish abundance of our consumer society comes at ever steeper costs. Critics and theorists do take note.)

Interestingly, some of the most recognized critics of the reengineered US higher education system and its downsizing of the academic workforce hold (or have held) distinguished positions and endowed chairs. I am thinking, for example, of Michael Bérubé, John Guillory, Cary Nelson, Andrew Ross, and Stanley Aronowitz. As possessors of the last good job in America, they have developed their applied vernacular theories by attending characteristically to the grim situation of casual labor, especially new Ph.D.s seeking jobs, the graduate students they work with day in day out. Structurally speaking, the distinguished professor is an enviable person, a model, a position to aspire to, yet – given current altered circumstances – also something of a cover, fig leaf, delusory figure, justifying at once meritocracy, a prestige economy, hard work, productivity, false promises. The distinguished professor these days presides, knowingly or not, at the top of Nelson's pyramid scheme. Yet the main point is not that some people are well employed, but that too many are under- and unemployed. During recent years it has been the plight mainly of casualized labor to raise consciousness and organize protests. In these circumstances distinguished professors have often been a hindrance, as in the Yale strike (with exceptions); sometimes a help, as with the labor theorists at hand; but largely above the fray, a position increasingly less tenable.

What is to be done? Here let me provide a condensed version of a broad array of recommendations culled from the current literature on the academic employment situation. Naturally, inconsistencies appear. Cap casual labor at 15 percent for each institution. Pay $6,000–8,000 per course to adjuncts (not the usual $2,000). Unite all disciplinary organizations in advocating on behalf of casual labor. Stop the conversion of full-time tenure-track jobs to casual labor. (Re)convert contingent to full-time tenure-track jobs.[27] Redefine "faculty" to include casual workers. Inform potential graduate students about the job situation. Shorten the time to the Ph.D. degree. Increase fellowships for Ph.D. students. Freeze admissions to Ph.D. programs for, say, five years. Eliminate and cut back Ph.D. programs. Reduce TA work loads to no more than one course per semester or year (instead of the typical three, four, or five courses per year). Renounce the apprenticeship in favor of the employee model of TA work. Establish collective bargaining units for faculty, including casual workers. Insure decent wages, benefits, pension contributions, job security, free speech rights, and a role in governance for casualized as well as regular faculty. Encourage employment outside academe for new Ph.D.s. Facilitate retirements. Return to mandatory retirement.[28] Replace all retirements with full-time tenure-track positions. Hire academically oriented administrators (avoid compliant bottom-line pragmatists). Disseminate censure lists of high casual labor programs and schools. Publish part-time versus full-time faculty ratios as well as student–teacher ratios for all institutions, making the information available on a regular basis to faculty, staff, students, parents, alumni, trustees, legislators, and the public. Privatize severely underfunded public colleges and universities. Create debt forgiveness programs for students. Promote the 30-hour work week. Stop emulating corporations. Oppose the neoliberal addiction to low wages and exploitation of workers. If I had to choose just three from these several dozen recommendations, they would be: pay $6,000–8,000 per course to adjuncts; reduce TA work to one course per year; unionize workers.

What is visibly at stake here is the future of a profession. I came to realize this in an unexpected way when in 1997, the year I received an endowed chair, my oldest child entered an M.A. program and asked my advice about pursuing a Ph.D. and an academic career. She worked as a TA for two years, closely observing the situation of her peers and professors and ultimately deciding against becoming a professor. Wise choice, I thought. This decision was a relief to me, but a disappointment too. Given the situation of US higher education today, pursuing a Ph.D. and an academic career is, in many fields, high risk behavior. I would not have wished to say so fifteen years ago, still hoping that swelling enrollments and coming retirements might add up to good job prospects. Expectations die hard, but they do die.

Part III
Literature

At present American poetry is so vast and diverse as to be virtually unknowable.

Twentieth-Century American Poetry (2004)

Any version of the *local* or *regional* . . . will thus have to be spread on some cognitive map of *global postmodernity*.

Rob Wilson, *Reimagining the American Pacific* (2000)

Part III of *Living with Theory* maps the postmodern disorganization of literature, detailing the many expansive effects on it of multiculturalism, popular culture, and globalization. In its two case studies, propounded from the perspective of a theory-informed and classroom-attuned cultural studies, it documents the contemporary interest in minor literatures and genres, in porous national borders and transnational literary formations, and in the roles occupied by vernacular and vanguard traditions. Since the 1970s, feminist, ethnic, and postcolonial theories have effectively foregrounded literature by women, people of color, and a wide range of subalterns, altering literary history and university literature teaching. While *Living with Theory* takes account of these and other dramatic positive changes, it sheds light on and worries: the structural transformation of literature into entertainment; the growing burdens of literary abundance; and the attenuations of literature's socially critical powers. Along the way it foregrounds the role both criticism and literature play today in projects of nation-building and maintenance.

7

Late Contemporary US Poetry

Contemporary US poetry has a history distinct from that of fiction and drama. The usual accounts feature a variegated historical sequence of schools and movements from World War Two to the present: Academic Formalism, Objectivism, Black Mountain, San Francisco Renaissance, New York Poets, Beats, Confessionalism, Deep Image and Surrealism, Black Aesthetics, Ethnopoetics, Women's Poetry, Concrete Poetry, Language Poetry, New Formalism. This standard list leaves out an array of recent phenomena such as slam, rap, cowboy poetry, and digital poetics, not to mention the background poetry of popular music like blues, folk, country, and rock. Given this abundance, contemporary poets appear more fractious yet also more communal than novelists and dramatists. Not surprisingly, the US poetry field strikes many critics as increasingly carnivalesque and chaotic. If there is a center or axis, it is probably represented by the University of Iowa Writers' Workshop poem. This is the self-consciously prosaic confessional lyric of 20–40 free-verse lines, a longtime favorite of classroom teachers and magazine editors, who particularly appreciate its brevity, approachability, sincerity, and epiphanic wisdom. Firmly associated with the numerous university creative writing programs, the M.F.A. poem embodies for many critics a certain academic mainstream, which it has done for four decades.[1] Starting in the 1950s the US university has continued to offer poets steady jobs. The workshop poem remains a norm and a target, providing a sense of coherence to the otherwise disorganized field of late contemporary US poetry.

This chapter surveys the many contending practices and theories of poetry in the US during the postmodern period from the perspective of the present moment of maximum fragmentation of the field. It uses the wide-ranging conservative accounts of Dana Gioia, among the most provocative and insightful of American poet-critics writing today, to help map the terrain and lay out key issues. Not uncritically, it discusses the role of academic creative writing; of "opposing poetries"; of new poetry scenes and networks; and of the crisis of the lyric "I." The situation of poetry today has a great deal to say about the status of literature in early twenty-first century US society, concerning not only its vitality and abundance, but also its disarray and confusion as well as its ongoing transformation into entertainment and marketable product. Meanwhile, academe continues to value poetry as personal expression, finely crafted artifact, historical document, culturally symptomatic discourse, and national showpiece.

Poet–critic Mark Wallace suggests there are nowadays five "networks of US poetry production": (1) formalism; (2) confessionalism; (3) identity-based verse; (4) speech-oriented poetics; and (5) the avant-garde.[2] This matrix possesses the twin virtues of simplicity and scope, although the five networks overlap. As a matter of fact, they interact in complicated ways not just with the many existing schools and movements, but with geographical regions, creative writing programs, multicultural politics, and performance aesthetics. Numerous permutations and odd combinations exist as, for example, the identity-based confessional oral works of the Beats, of Black Arts poetry, and of some New York poets (such as Frank O'Hara and Edward Field). In the absence of a dominant school or looming major figure or text like T. S. Eliot's *The Waste Land*, the field of present-day US poetry reveals its identity as gaudy dispersion. Some critics have thus given up talk of "poetry" altogether in favor of "poetries," accepting the incommensurabilities characteristic of today's broad poetic universe. If one adds to the account the presence of three generations publishing at any given moment, still more stratifications emerge. As I write in 2007, for instance, Richard Wilbur (born 1921), Sharon Olds (1942), and Sherman Alexie

(1966) are esteemed and productive US poets. Wilbur is a formalist celebrated since the 1950s, Olds a confessionalist who hit her full stride in the 1980s, and Alexie a spoken-word identity-based poet bursting on the scene in the 1990s. This cameo only hints at the dispersion of the poetic field at the start of the twenty-first century.

"Postmodernism" generally names the disorganization of the cultural field since the 1970s.[3] Among the widely attested and relevant features that characterize the postmodern period are the rise of the new social movements, especially women's and ethnic civil rights; the recognition of multiculturalism as social reality; the collapse of the high/low cultural divide; the erosion of autonomous spheres, including aesthetic realms; the emergence of heterogeneous assemblages such as happenings, rock operas, and "long poems" (that is, sequences of discontinuous pieces); and the deconstruction of the modern Cartesian subject. While disaggregation is the most salient feature, it takes on singular configurations in the case of late contemporary US poetry.

In one major anthology, *Twentieth-Century American Poetry* (2004), the well-informed editors note "The contemporary poetry world is highly factionalized and combative; numerous aesthetic, ideological, professional, and regional camps busily make a critical case for their own creative enterprise. . . . At present American poetry is so vast and diverse as to be virtually unknowable."[4] The more upbeat and broadly focused editors of the best-selling *Heath Anthology of American Literature*, 5th edition, published in 2006, stress the diversity, pluralization, and disarray of contemporary US literature in general, speculating that "the very decentering of American literature has made it more integral to international culture."[5] And the editors of the *Norton Anthology of Modern and Contemporary Poetry*, 3rd edition of 2003, contrast modern and postmodern, observing "The poetry of our time is characterized by its pluralism, by its welter and crosscurrents. No longer can any single group or individual claim centrality."[6]

It is worth recalling in passing that the history of modernist American poetry from the period 1910s–1940s continues to be reconfigured from various postmodernist points of view, a revisionist enterprise initiated in earnest during the 1970s and continuing today. Recent anthologies contain, for example, many more poems by women and ethnic and politically radical writers than those of the early Cold War era. This is noticeably the case with Oxford University Press's *Anthology of Modern American Poetry*, edited by Cary Nelson and published in 2000, which covers the long twentieth century from Whitman to Alexie. Among its many surprises are wall poems from anonymous Chinese immigrants housed in Angel Island Detention Center and haiku from World War Two concentration camps for Japanese Americans. This is not your grandfather's modernist American poetry, the canonical Pound-Eliot-Williams-Frost-Stevens line, with some Amy Lowell and H.D. thrown in. It is multiracial, multiethnic, multiclass, transnational and, by implication, multilingual.

The sense of poetry's present state of postmodern disaggregation can arguably best be gleaned from Dana Gioia's recent essay collections on US poetry, *Disappearing Ink: Poetry at the End of Print Culture* (2004), as well as his earlier infamous *Can Poetry Matter? Essays on Poetry and American Culture* (1992). In his best-known articles Gioia (pronounced joy-a) vigorously champions traditional poetry, that is, popular realist strands as represented by Longfellow, Frost, Jeffers, Bishop, and Kooser. These poets use rhyme and meter, clear language, engaging stories, and characters accessible to the common reader. Gioia promotes narrative over lyric. He scorns the modernist avant-gardes, usually by implication or omission. He rarely mentions the Pound-Stein-Williams-H.D. line of experimental poets that leads to contemporary Language poetry, which peaked in the 1980s and 1990s, a time when Gioia, born in 1950, was coming onto the scene and advocating the contending New Formalism. Gioia excoriates the workshop poem and the creative writing establishment. In his account the latter has for 40 years promoted prosaic free verse and brief narcissistic lyrics, all the while setting up exclusionary institutions and lapsing into cronyism.

In the cultural wars and literary politics of the past two decades, Gioia is a conservative, defending tradition and standards, a scourge

106

of a bloated and predictable academe, a promoter of the common reader, and a critic of obscurantist vanguardism. Author of three books of criticism, three books of poetry, translator of books by the poets Montale and Seneca, and editor or coeditor of more than a dozen books, half of them textbooks, Dana Gioia is arguably the leading poet-critic and public intellectual poet of his generation.[7] He was appointed in 2003 to the chairmanship of the National Endowment for the Arts, a consecration never before experienced by an American poet during the 40-year history of the NEA. In 2004 he published the coedited volumes *Twentieth-Century American Poetry* and *Twentieth-Century American Poetics: Poets and the Art of Poetry*, among the best textbooks in the field. They are comprehensive, scholarly, and student friendly, solidifying his standing as a chief arbiter of US poetry today.

Published in 1991 by the *Atlantic Monthly*, Gioia's most notorious essay "Can Poetry Matter?" had such an impact that it allowed him to quit his job of 15 years as a marketing executive for General Foods in New York and to go back home to California to become a full-time writer. During the 1970s he earned a Master's degree in comparative literature at Harvard University. After that he returned to his alma mater, Stanford University, where he took an M.B.A. So he was a businessman-poet in the formative years of his career. There is a long American line of such poets extending from Eliot, Stevens, and Williams to MacLeish, Eberhart, Ammons, and Dickey to Hugo, Ingnatow, Bronk, and Kooser. Like some of them, Gioia felt himself an outsider in the literary world. The alienation of the employed nonprofessional poet, he argues, produces a certain maturity and realism, allowing time to grow in contrast to the mad, sometimes suicidal rush experienced by the hungry literary freelancer or the academic poet facing high publish-or-perish quotas. Neither bohemian nor scholar, the American businessman-poet, laments Gioia, has not written of business topics nor much about the real world, addressing the self and thereby contributing to the loss of public language and broader audiences for poetry.[8]

Gioia's populism – the motivating force behind "Can Poetry Matter?" – stems like all populism from a dislike of elites. In his case, they consist of four groups: the academic poetry establishment; obscurantist, often haughty avant-gardists (that category includes literary theorists); unnamed political progressives; and partisan and subjective book reviewers. He positions himself as a man of the people, a nonacademic, nonbohemian, sensible business person, devoted to traditions of popular poetry, disinterested critical analysis, and the general reader.

What most characterizes late contemporary US poetry during the fin de siècle, according to Gioia, is that it belongs to a specialized subculture housed in the university and removed from society and intellectual life. Paradoxically, it proliferates in quantitative terms of published books, grants, awards, public readings, creative writing programs, journals, jobs, writer's colonies, scholarly criticism, and subsidies. Wedded to the university and no longer to urban bohemia, it faces inward not outward, losing connection and influence on society. This makes it different from contemporary fiction, which retains a broad audience and has widely recognized writers and frequent coverage in the media.

Gioia recalls Edmund Wilson long ago pointed out, in "Is Verse a Dying Technique?" (1934), that since the eighteenth century poetry has gradually given up narrative, drama, satire, and history, retreating to lyric and turning over much ground to prose. More recently, notes Gioia, Joseph Epstein in "Who Killed Poetry?" (1988) contrasted the substantial achievements of modernist poets with the far less significant accomplishments of contemporary professional poets now ensconced in the university. By the 1990s the audience for poetry had condensed to a professional "loyal coterie" (*CPM*, p. 5), losing the nonspecialist readers and outlets of earlier decades. What little poetry reviewing exists is nowadays done largely by friendly specialists, not a general press and mainly for the purposes of publicity rather than disinterested assessment. According to Gioia, the same lack of criticism and of standards of quality mars poetry anthologizing. In publish-or-perish academe, quantity rather than quality counts. Dull, mediocre, and bad poems are ubiquitous, a product of the poetry industry. The mission of the professional poet is education not art; he or she addresses students not the whole of humanity. Estranged from literary historians and critics, poets dwell in departmental enclaves as isolated specialists talking to one another.

Midway in his harangue Gioia offers several pages contrasting the standing of US poetry in 1940 to that of 1990. He creates a narrative of decline, appearing the traditional conservative decrying the times and harkening back to better days. Back then few poets taught in universities. Only one creative writing program existed (the Iowa Writer's Workshop). Poets survived as business people, literary journalists, freelancers, urban bohemians, or rural holdouts. A hundred new poetry books appeared annually compared with several thousand nowadays. Books were widely reviewed. The monthly magazine *Poetry* covered the whole field. Reviewers were "extraordinarily tough" (*CPM*, p. 13), being loyal to readers and not to fellow poets nor publishers. Among the dozen precursor public intellectual poet-critics singled out for admiration by Gioia one finds John Ciardi, Langston Hughes, Randall Jarrell, Kenneth Rexroth, Delmore Schwartz, and Yvor Winters, all of whom addressed a broad intelligentsia, an audience now lost. "Poetry mattered outside the classroom" (*CPM*, p. 16).

Gioia's diagnosis of the situation of late contemporary US poetry attains levels of severity and incendiary tones in a few telling passages such as these two:

> Like subsidized farming that grows food no one wants, a poetry industry has been created to serve the interests of producers and not the consumers. And in the process the integrity of the art has been betrayed. Of course no poet is allowed to admit this in public. The cultural credibility of the professional poetry establishment depends on maintaining a polite hypocrisy. (*CPM*, p. 8)

> Today poetry is a modestly upwardly mobile, middle-class profession – not as lucrative as waste management or dermatology but several big steps above the squalor of bohemia. (*CPM*, p. 11)

These barbs are aimed at creative writers in the universities coming from the outsider Gioia, who here appears in a leading intellectual

109

monthly. Warehoused in the university, contemporary poetry does not matter to the general public. Its subsidies, parochialisms, and hypocrisies call for reform as well as condemnation and alarm.

The task of poetry today, as Gioia sees it, is fourfold: reconnect with a wide audience; address broad issues; keep the language clear and healthy; and join the other arts, now isolated and fragmented, in disseminating high culture (*CPM*, p. 18). Above all, poetry professionals should go public, leaving behind the "intellectual ghetto" and "stuffy classroom" (*CPM*, p. 21).

A few years ago Dana Gioia offered yet another wide-ranging overview and assessment of the state of US poetry in the title essay to his collection *Disappearing Ink: Poetry at the End of Print Culture*. This report of 2004 is surprisingly upbeat in the face of all the growing anxieties concerning the recent triumph of electronic media over print culture and the ongoing antiquation of serious literature. The most significant fact about poetry in America during the past quarter-century, observes Gioia now, has been "the wide-scale and unexpected reemergence of popular poetry – namely, rap, cowboy poetry, poetry slams, and... performance poetry."[9] These forms of poetry thrive outside academic networks and are disconnected from modernism, the avant-gardes, and most of the recognized schools and movements of the postwar period. Not linked to the printed page, the new popular poetry has received little attention from "official verse culture," to use Charles Bernstein's famous term.[10] Tellingly, it is not suited to mainstream critical analysis in the scholarly manners of leading critics like Helen Vendler or Harold Bloom, both of whom focus on isolated geniuses and the great tradition. Meanwhile, the overheated attention of the media has attended to celebrity, money, and human foibles. It has missed the new popular poetry's "radical innovation and unorthodox traditionalism" (*DI*, p. 8), as well as its reconfiguration of the modes of poetry production, circulation, and consumption.

During the course of his tableau, Gioia notes in passing that he employs the term "poetry" in an "all-inclusive sense to include all forms of verse – written or oral – that shape language for literary

110

effect," doing so because the term "now encompasses so many diverse and often irreconcilable artistic enterprises" (*DI*, p. 8). *Literary* poetry in his usage refers to written high-art work, while *popular* poetry names the forms of verse outside official channels. Explicitly, he brackets the issue of quality, a sensible move for a populist but an odd tactic for a defender of the great tradition. Surprisingly, Gioia joins cultural studies scholars here, faithful to his baby boomer generation that accepts popular arts as serious culture.

Dana Gioia highlights four broad differences between today's popular and literary poetries. It's a mixed story. First, the new popular poetries are oral (not written), meaning spoken and often improvisational. Thus they are capable of reaching a national audience via recordings, radio, television, concerts, and festivals. Not surprisingly, they have turned the poet into an entertainer. Second, the new popular poetries stem from the margins rather than the mainstream. Rap comes from the ghetto; cowboy poetry from rural America; and slam from urban environments. The lumpen class orientations of popular poetry clash with the middle-class literary establishment's poetry. Interestingly, rap resuscitates certain forms of folk culture; cowboy poetry revives the pastoral genre; and slam recalls the declamatory poetry competitions of ancient times. Third, these new popular poetries are "formal," meaning they use meter and rhyme. Also, they favor narrative, a discredited genre in the modern age of the lyric. So a huge gap has opened between the free-verse print culture of the literati's workshop poetry and the jangling orality of the popular poets steeped in humanity's primal pleasure in verbal music and employing the alliterated and assonantal four-stress accentual lines, couplets, and ballad forms of old. Fourth, the new popular poetries are profitable, thriving with neither state, private, nor academic subsidies and attracting large audiences.

In midcourse Gioia reverses direction in "Disappearing Ink," arguing that slowly but surely literary poetry is heeding popular poetry. "In a society with too many books and too little time for reading, especially serious literary reading, a book of poems, no matter how superb, can no longer be sure of attracting an audience by means of print alone" (*DI*, p. 21). The public poetry reading has metamorphosed into the main way that literary poets nowadays reach wide audiences beyond small book-buying readerships. Gioia contrasts the modernist poets, who rarely gave public readings and then only late during their careers, with contemporary poets starting with the Beats and culminating with Billy Collins, US Poet Laureate in 2001, who made his name by public readings on radio and in lecture halls. Significantly, Gioia now sees the more or less unified enterprise of high-art, literary poetry fragmenting into four sketchy forms unconnected to any earlier specific contemporary school or movement, whose days are in any case almost over. They are performance poetry, spoken-word poetry, audiovisual poetry, and visual poetry.

In the field of twenty-first century US literary poetry, argues Gioia, "performance poetry" merges traditions of oral poetry, improvisational theatre, and standup comedy. It forsakes print altogether for video and audio recording. For its part "spoken-word poetry," while being performative, maintains links with words and sounds more than with the body and space of the performer. Such work is similar to rap, slam, and cowboy verse. "Audiovisual poetry" extends modernist impulses in creating words that function as both typographic and spoken texts. But it stays closer to oral rhythms and clear music than to the syntax and rhetoric of print. And "visual poetry" more or less deemphasizes orality in favor of typography by using silent reading as its model and often space and page design as key values. Gioia associates this visual work unfavorably with Black Mountain, Concrete, and Language vanguardist poetries. Most significantly, he concedes that today's poets mix and match the four forms more or less freely, testifying to the phenomena of postmodern pluralism, pastiche, and fusion.

The print culture of literary poetry is in decline: that is Dana Gioia's main argument. Here is his big picture. Within the US university, poetry has sadly ceded status to literary theory and cultural studies. Academic poetry criticism exists as a mandarin enterprise. Poetry review outlets, often little magazines, are inaccessible to most readers. And in any case reviews are bland and uncritical. The campus poetry reading, on the other hand, is alive and well. But in the absence of broad media coverage it remains a decidedly local affair, even though it does make poetry books available for sale in a way that many bookstores still do not. "The forty-year period of undisputed dominance that the university exercised over American poetry... is now over. American poetry is presently returning to a more historically typical, and intellectually healthier situation where the university's role is balanced by a strong nonacademic literary culture" (*DI*, pp. 26–7). Provocatively, Gioia observes that an emerging "new bohemia" has a key role to play in the historical rebalancing of the poetic field.

Like previous ones, the new bohemia, stresses Gioia, is made up of independent, generally nonprofit publishers, small reviewing magazines, service organizations, garage producers (especially desktop publishers), and literature-friendly institutions. The latter include bookstores, community centers, libraries, museums, art galleries, plus schools, many of which nowadays regularly welcome poets and poetry readings. Not located in one urban enclave but scattered across many metroplexes, the new bohemia is connected as much by electronic media as communal space. Among nonacademic noncommercial presses cited by Gioia are Copper Canyon, Curbstone, Graywolf (his publisher), and Story Line; the zines/networks include *Contemporary Poetry Review, Eratosphere*, and *Poetry Daily*; the organizations named are Academy of American Poets, Poets House, Poetry Society of America, and Poets & Writers. These lists could be amplified to cover a much broader range of poetries. The paradigmatic institution of the new bohemia for Gioia is the thriving literary bookstore shaped in the past two decades by an "entrepreneurial vanguard" in the work of marketing ideas and experiences as well as books. Bookstores regularly employ oral cultural forms such as readings, interviews, discussion groups, and lectures in an egalitarian atmosphere. Paradoxically, the American university has contributed to bohemia by turning out 25,000 M.F.A.s each decade. The many jobless graduates often join the ranks of bohemia, staffing bookstores, presses, zines, newspapers, community centers, online poetry networks, and arts organizations. This creates checks and balances between academia and bohemia. "Because the new bohemia is so decentralized, few people, including its own members, now realize the scope of its activities. . . . Today, for the first time in fifty years, the vast majority of young American writers now live and work outside the university" (*DI*, p. 29).

In the conclusion to "Disappearing Ink," Gioia argues in a suggestive though self-interested way that New Formalists (with whom he has been identified since the mid-1980s), along with slam, rap, cowboy, and spoken-word poets, "constitute an auditory avant-garde" (*DI*, p. 29). This is not a matter of a poetic school or a movement, but a broad "shift in sensibility," a "change in the *Zeitgeist*," a "widespread and decentralized response to the new oral culture" (*DI*, p. 29). Included in this heterogeneous phenomenon are academic and bohemian poets; young and old; political progressives, conservatives, and anarchists; experimentalists and traditionalists. The new popular traditionalist oral poetry appears to be reenlivening academic literary poetry, although academic poetry critics with their retrograde modernist perspectives seem oblivious. "The relation between print and speech in American culture today is probably closer to that in Shakespeare's age than Eliot's era – not an altogether bad situation for a poet" (*DI*, p. 31). It is even possible that poetry is better positioned to thrive in an oral culture than the novel. Gioia is upbeat and guardedly optimistic at the outset of the new century.

Dana Gioia wants and welcomes revolution. In *Disappearing Ink* he sketches a theory of poetic revolutions to account for our times:

> Every thirty or forty years a significant shift occurs in poetic sensibility. The change usually takes the form of a generational revolt as young poets reject the dominant style of their elders. Twentieth-century American poetry has seen at least three upheavals. The first came shortly before World War I when early Modernists like Ezra Pound, T. S. Eliot, Wallace Stevens, and H. D. renounced the softness and sentimentality of late Victorian verse. The second seismic shift came just after midcentury when the Beat and Confessional poets abandoned

the decorous impersonality and stylistic formalism of the New Critical aesthetic. The third upheaval is happening right now as various camps of populist poetry attack an increasingly tired and fragmented academic subculture. (*DI*, p. 229)

There are some noteworthy concessions as well as implications buried in this quick sketch. In attacking academic poetry in the past, Gioia cast it as unified, but here he portrays it as fragmented, which is much truer to reality. Populist poetry is divided into camps, and beyond that it consists of local "scenes": the new bohemia, though networked, comes out of scattered metroplexes. In my own locale, Oklahoma City, there are a half dozen weekly poetry readings, some hosted by arts organizations, some by coffee shops, and some by bars. Bookstores, both chains and independents, regularly hold poetry events, as do several of the universities in the area, especially the ones with creative writing programs. There is a rap scene located in clubs as well as separate roots, country, blues, and post-punk alternative scenes. In the case of the blues, which I have written about elsewhere, there are local factions, not surprisingly, but closer to the point a handful of superior song writers and song interpreters.[11] Things are more complicated and atomized than Gioia suggests here not only about literary academia and the new artistic bohemia, but also about US poetic revolutions.

Poetic revolutions are not just a matter of young generations rebelling against reigning styles, but of artists discovering enabling precursors, plus developing new standpoints, political positions, worldviews, languages, and forms, and throwing off constraints of various worldly as well as artistic sorts. The concept of altered "sensibility" doesn't capture this complexity. Also, revolutions don't pit A against B, but involve C, D, and E, even if history telling gravitates toward the clearer plot of A to B. What does one say, for example, of early twentieth-century proletarian poetry? Or of poetry by women and ethnic writers of that time? Not to mention Gioia's much-admired regional poetry? The history of the modern revolution in US poetry includes ethnic modernisms, regional currents and countercurrents, previously disregarded proletarian and women writers, overlooked

115

popular poetries and song traditions, as well as widely recognized avant-gardes, often transatlantic, sometimes broadly Europeanized, occasionally orientalist. Literary histories have a great deal to account for, including losers as well as winners. A new history of postmodernist poetic revolution that pits triumphant popular poetries against an entrenched academic creative writing subculture or broader literary poetry is Manichean and simplistic, however memorable and dramatic. Popular poetry is a differentiated universe; so too is academic poetry. Perversely, vanguard poetries like Language poetry and digital poetry do not even register in the history of late contemporary US poetry that Gioia outlines.[12]

Despite being captivating and wide-ranging, there are then serious problems with Dana Gioia's various tableaux of US poetry today. There is much more atomization, tension, and noncommunication or lack of contact among the multitude of poetry scenes, camps, schools, movements, and subcultures. *Pace* Gioia, academe still represents a mainstream, garnering many public resources and recognitions. Black hole or bright spot, academic poetry remains a key center of the expanding poetry universe.

It is telling that Gioia lately gives up critical evaluation in the face of contemporary poetry's ongoing proliferation. In the past his brand of critical disinterest designated Arnoldian tough quality judgments in line with canonical touchstones instead of his new stance of historical impartiality and cultural relativism. The purported triumph of popular poetries over academe's monopoly perhaps reveals more about the depth of Gioia's personal resentment as an outsider than about the actual lay of the land. Belatedly and surprisingly, Gioia swerves to cultural studies here marked variously by his celebration of mass popular culture (both low- and middle-brow); his bracketing of aesthetic judgment; his focus on cultural circuits of production, distribution, and consumption; and his positioning himself as a public intellectual rather than a disinterested mandarin critic or a connoisseur. However, he considers neither the social roots, nor the surrounding context, nor the content of popular poetries (such as gangsta rap). He prefers to stress above all else the return of form, especially meter

116

and rhyme. What is arguably most interesting in the popular poetries of recent years is less the obvious rhythm, rhyme, and new orality than the revealing social valences, the signifying accoutrements, and the messages. But whether motivated by resentment against academic poetry or by recently much broadened conceptions of poetry as well as criticism, Dana Gioia's map of the US poetry world at the opening of the twenty-first century merits praise for its openness to popular culture, despite its other limitations.

A key element of Gioia's story, composed over the course of a quarter-century, is a marked crisis of the reader. His default assumption is that there is a "common reader" whom he equates occasionally with the general and the educated reader. In other people's treatments these three are rarely the same, an issue dealt with in chapter 3. Gioia the populist wants poetry to address and to reach the common reader. We know from histories of literacy and of the book, not to mention reader-response theory, that the common reader is a myth. But consider the following odd statement: "The great Modernists like Pound, Eliot, Cummings, and Stevens demonstrated how powerfully complex poetry can speak to the common reader" (*DI*, 256). Ezra Pound speaking to the common reader? At the mall? Well, no! It turns out Gioia's common readers belong to the highly educated cultural elite composing roughly 2 percent of the US population: "Representing our cultural intelligentsia, they are the people who support the arts – who buy classical and jazz records; who attend foreign films, serious theatre, opera, symphony, and dance; who read quality fiction and biographies. . . . If one accepts the conservative estimate that it accounts for only 2 percent of the US population, it still represents a potential audience of almost five million readers" (*CPM*, p. 16). With all this specific cultural capital in their possession, it is clear such "common" readers do not regularly buy country and blues CDs, watch TV or Hollywood movies, listen to AM radio, attend rock concerts, or read pulp fiction. So it seems an abuse of language for Gioia to use the word "common" to describe this rarefied upper crust. His elitist populism, however, very much depends on this mystified usage here and elsewhere.

117

Sooner or later the truth will out: "the continuous proliferation of information has increasingly fragmented audiences into specialized subcultures that share no common frame of reference" (*CPM*, p. 222). Indeed. So much for the chimerical "common reader." Appearing now and then in Gioia's criticism, the key figure of the common reader operates three symptomatic ways. It prompts lamentation about the good old days as well as the fragmented present. It holds out the promise of some day unifying the heterogeneous poetic fields. Most importantly, it powers Gioia's elitist populism. Significantly, the poetry of the twenty-first century's revolutionary new bohemia, according to Gioia's very recent altered view, is popular rather than literary poetry, free from the print page and accessible to mass audiences beyond so-called common readers. The implication is that poets should address this new audience, using all the resources of traditional formal verse, seeking clarity and accessibility, and maximum exposure. The shift from the common reader to the mass audience marks a profound change in Gioia's writings on US poetry today.

It is perhaps no surprise that as a declared New Formalist, Dana Gioia has nothing to say about postindustrial society, laissez-faire capitalism, or globalization. One would expect, nevertheless, that the poet–critic as engaged public intellectual would be more explicit and direct on current economics, politics, and society, as well as the arts. One wonders if he believes the contemporary disorganization of US poetry entails any political or economic losses. How is it related to third wave or late capitalism? Is cooptation a problem? What about commodification? Is the restructuring of poetry into entertainment a positive change? Is there a critical role for poetry? Do narrative poems and long poems circumvent the narcissism of the contemporary mainstream self-expressive lyric? All these issues seem very far away. Much nearer to hand is the celebration of all manner of popular poetries (old and new) and of bohemias (old and new), with half-hearted ill-informed scattered jabs at three enemies: the creative writing establishment, avant-gardes, and literary theory. Most significantly, no consideration is given as to whether or not the new popular poetries constitute bread and circuses, that is, entertainment and distraction from the real political economic business of restructuring, downsizing, and privatizing in line with the contemporary neoliberal project to dismantle the US welfare state. What has been going on during the time Gioia has been writing? Silence.

Dana Gioia has nothing to say about Anglophone poetry. There is no mention of Kamau Brathwaithe, Seamus Heaney, Les Murray, A. K. Ramanujan, Wole Soyinka, or Derek Walcott. He appears very much a provincial nationalist in this and other regards. *Disappearing Ink* and *Can Poetry Matter?* focus exclusively on US poetry. Gioia's third book of criticism, *Barrier of a Common Language: An American Looks at Contemporary British Poetry* (2003), records the postwar divorce of British and American poetry from a self-declared alien US standpoint. "British poetry" is here defined to include English, Welsh, Scottish, and Cornish English-language writers, but not Irish (Northern or Southern). The heartfelt and nuanced appreciations of Philip Larkin, Charles Causley, James Fenton, Wendy Cope, and others are from a self-asserted outsider's point of view. Gioia's main argument is that we live in "an age when American and British English are drifting further apart."[13] But surely part of the story of late contemporary US poetry, itself already a mixture of postcolonial poetries, is its embeddedness in global Anglophone networks and not simply its national proliferation, atomization, and apparent isolation. Gioia overlooks all contemporary international, transnational, multi-lingual, and multicultural poetries and poetics such as black aesthetics, feminism, indigenous and ethno-poetics, neo-surrealism, confession-alism, testimonial and prison poetries, digital poetics. The Black Atlantic, Pacific Basin, and Americas make no appearance. There is no mention of the landmark two-volume global anthology *Poems for the Millennium* (1995, 1998), edited by Jerome Rothenberg and Pierre Joris. For Gioia the imaginary borders around the US evidently are thick and high. As a scholar of comparative literature, a child of immigrants (Sicilian and Mexican grandparents), and a trans-lator from several languages, his three books of criticism strangely exhibit a nationalist mindset. This unfortunately blinds him to a great deal of what is going on in, through, and around US poetry.

119

A major battleground of contemporary poetry and poetics as well as of literary and cultural theory is the crisis of subjectivity. Dana Gioia is of no help here and must be left behind at this point. The human subject of official verse culture is invariably a solitary, sincere, expressive self, exhibiting a stable unified identity and a unique organic voice focused on intimate experiences and personal insights. This is a notion of self fit for the possessive individualism of contemporary consumer society, often narcissistic, emotive, sentimental, privatized in the extreme. The cult of the personal poetic voice is most obvious in the neoconfessionalism that dominates M.F.A. workshop poetry, but it also runs through much nonacademic work. Here is a recent characterization from leading poetry critic Marjorie Perloff: "Most poetry currently written continues to follow the basic assumptions that govern the works.... A generic 'sensitive' lyric speaker contemplates a facet of his or her world and makes observations about it, compares present to past, divulges some hidden emotion, or comes to a new understanding of the situation."[14] Such formula poetry, which Perloff accurately labels "typical subjective realism," depends on an isolated, coherent, self-absorbed subject most easily spotted in the gated communities of the suburbs.

The much-discussed postmodern deconstruction of the self stems from four broad theoretical fields. First, psychoanalysis and its artistic offshoot surrealism install an unconscious that questions self-understanding and rationality. Both movements credit the role of psychic distortions like repression and projection in the constitution of the subject whose discourse is molded by unconscious forces. Second, the new social movements, especially women's and various civil rights ones, show the self to be gendered and racialized as well as part of class society. Thus it is necessary to talk about occupying multiple subject positions collectively configured (such as poor black gay woman, middle-class white heterosexual male, etc.). Postcolonial theory here adds national identity as fundamental to subject formation. Third, linguistic theories argue that language speaks humankind, that syntax shapes rationality, that discourse is dialogical and heteroglot, and that signifiers slide, most notably in the process of self-constitution.

120

In this context, theory of performative language underlines the essential role of social conventions, rituals, and posing in the formation of subjectivity. Fourth, cyborg theory of technoscience foregrounds the often unrecognized fundamental role of numerous technologies in the development of the contemporary posthuman self. These technologies range from pharmaceuticals, childhood immunizations, and treated water and air to modified foods and supplements, to prostheses like dental work and body replacement parts to surveillance mechanisms and communication devices. All help in forming a post-organic technicized cyborg subject integrated into social circuitry. The net effect of these deconstructions is the decentering of the modern Cartesian subject ("I think, therefore, I am"), revealed now to be presocial, naively disembodied, irrational, monological, ahistorical, mystified, nostalgic. In any event, it is unfit for poetry in our time.

In his meditation "On Lyric Poetry and Society," Theodor Adorno famously illustrated "that the lyric work is always the subjective expression of a social antagonism."[15] Many prominent scholars of late contemporary US poetry have elaborated on the social dynamics of lyric voice. Walter Kalaidjian shows how "challenges to poetry's survival in the age of advanced capitalism compel poets to jettison traditional assumptions about the lyric self and poetic autonomy, thus aligning verse with the social text of the contemporary American scene."[16] When Jed Rasula discusses the intertwined obstacles North American experimental poets have to confront, he lists them in this order: "the tyranny of the lyrical ego, the breath unit, the anecdote, the scenic moment, and the encumbering paraphernalia of authenticity."[17] The suggestion here that the lyric voice is a social construction with a peculiar embattled history receives elaboration from Michael Davidson. He demonstrates that today "the voice is not natural, that it is produced in a cultural marketplace among tape recorders, contact mikes, and phonetaps ... [being] an index for the way ideology speaks."[18] Such amplifications of the lyrical voice, which take into account the various historical conditions of its emergence, serve as background to Charles Altieri's generalization: poetry during postmodern times is constrained to "devote itself [1] to valuing the

121

imagination's powers to undo identities rather than to form them, [and 2] to feeding on contradiction and complexity rather than pursuing elegant, intricate syntheses."[19] Not only is the self a construct, but it is disjunctively so.

The deconstruction of the self manifests itself as thematic material (subject matter) more or less explicitly in experimental, multicultural, and speech-oriented poetics, but not so evidently in mainstream neoconfessional workshop poetry. Christopher Beach, for instance, observes:

> The effect of poetry slams and spoken-word performance has been not only to revitalize the oral and performative aspects of poetry... but also to resituate the personal. Instead of the lyric "I" as constituted within the postconfessional workshop poem – a voice that relies on a common understanding of the bourgeois suburban subject... – we find a voice that is more popularly constructed, often adopting a slang idiom while deemphasizing or parodying the "transcendent" or "sensitive" aspects of the lyric self and failing to provide the "revelatory" lyric moment.[20]

The personal is political complete with race, class, gender, national, and linguistic markers, conscious and unconscious: the late contemporary poetic self and its discourse cannot finally elude such dynamics in its staging. The humanist self of the dominant workshop poem is a particular historical formation, seeming ignorant of its privileges, its premises, its pasts. That is a key claim of much contemporary poetry scholarship.[21]

The subjects of late contemporary US theory, poetry, and culture respond to a society offering 300 television channels, official multiculturalism, and numerous competing incommensurable poetries. So many niches, so many commodities. The deconstruction of the subject corresponds to the proliferation and disaggregation characteristic of postmodern US society with its many and varied poetry schools, movements, camps, and scenes. It is no surprise that the poets have become individual entertainer-entrepreneurs and poetries commodities in glutted leisure and educational markets. Poets of all stripes are now part of the twenty-first century creative class embraced by chambers of commerce and urban planners, willingly or not.

Yet as poetry today partakes of community enacting dialogue with all its complex answerabilities, it reserves spaces for beleaguered poets capable of nay-saying, withdrawal, and criticism as well as entertainment, instruction, healing, art. Such performances are possible as occasion prompts, but in tandem and competition with other discourse producers and entertainers. The modernist image of the outsider bohemian solitary artist survives today as a charming compensatory nostalgic figure. The retro image of the renegade poet is ready to resurface anywhere at a moment's notice, only nowadays in the guise of a rapper, slam artist, rebel CEO, or NEA chairman.

8

Globalization of Literatures

My main observation in this final chapter is that conceptions of national literatures like American and British have changed dramatically since the 1960s and continue to do so today. Several factors are at work in these transformations. To begin with, minorities play a key role as literatures not only by women and "people of color," but by indigenous groups and immigrants are added to the canons of recognized texts. This raises tough questions about multiculturalism, including the place of minority languages, dialects, creoles, and pidgins in national literatures. In addition, previously ignored or discredited genres like diaries, slave and travel narratives, and aboriginal myths have in recent times been redignified and accepted as significant literary forms. The same is true, though to a lesser extent, for heretofore excluded genres of expanding popular culture as, for example, romance, Gothic horror, detective and science fiction. Moreover, formerly underappreciated regional formations such as the Black Atlantic, the Pacific Basin, and the Americas (spanning from Alaska to Argentina) have for a long time produced transnational literatures only recently being appreciated and studied. More broadly still, contemporary globalization has generated awareness of such postnational phenomena as Anglophone, Francophone, and Hispanophone literatures. My main point is that American and British literatures during postmodern globalized times, my lifetime, have entered into two states. First, there is a state of unprecedented expansion, following narrow contraction and purification during the mid twentieth-century formalist era dedicated to great works and precious craftsmanship. Second, there is a state of disaggregation, marked by the inclusion of marginal and transnational literatures and their sociohistorical worlds. Those changes have set the teaching matrix and academic departmentalization of literature into creative disarray, handled unevenly from one institution to another. All of these transformations bear very much upon current prospects for literary and cultural studies and upon living with theory today.

American Literature Now

How does the American literature of today compare with that of the 1960s before the transformations of recent decades? I studied American literature at three different US universities during the 1960s on my way to completing B.A., M.A., and Ph.D. programs in American and British literature. For me there are significant changes "within" and "without," if I can put it that way for purposes of illustration.

The changes "within" include cumulative additions to the canon of American literature, which is, of course, widely studied in the US university and elsewhere. These additions start with literary works by women and African Americans, followed by Hispanic, Native, and Asian Americans.[1] Many complications and theoretical questions have arisen here. Let me isolate the two most challenging. Given the hundreds of indigenous American Indian languages and the unwritten oral "literary" (often religious) forms of such works, mustn't the canon be expanded to include non-English languages as well as new genres? Moreover, will heretofore belletristic definitions of literature need to be further supplemented or jettisoned, making way for sociological and anthropological, not to mention historical, definitions?

With the appearance in 2000 of the landmark *Multilingual Anthology of American Literature: A Reader of Original Texts with English Translations*, edited by Marc Shell and Werner Sollors, two prominent Harvard literature professors, a reader discovers such non-English texts as *Walam Olum*, a Native American epic in pictographs of the

125

Delaware/Lanape language; an 1830s slave narrative in Arabic; an 1830s African American short story in French; an 1830s Italian American poem in Italian; a 1663 translation with annotations of the Bible into Massachusett, an Eastern Algonkian language; Chinese wall poems of the early twentieth century, found at Angel Island Detention Camp; Navajo songs and chants ("orature"); plus Euro-American literary texts in Danish, German, Greek, Hungarian, Norwegian, Polish, Spanish, Swedish, Welsh, and Yiddish. There are several poems in Germerican, a mixed language like Spanglish, Franglais, Chinglish, and Yinglish.[2] While American literature in the 1960s was a resolutely English-language only formation, today it is being reconstructed as a multilingual multicultural entity, with new genres as well as languages and dialects added. There is also a new literary history in the making that seeks to recover forgotten, suppressed, and lost works.

It goes without saying nowadays that the categories Hispanic and Asian American in the US, like Native American, require amplification. Hispanic includes Mexican, Puerto Rican, and Cuban American literatures, plus many Central and South American ones as well. By my count, the designation Asian American covers several dozen national traditions and languages, not only Chinese, Filipino/a, Japanese, and Korean, the big four historically speaking, but South and Southeast Asian, ranging from Pakistani and Indian to Cambodian and Vietnamese.

I have said nothing thus far about the uneven inclusion into the American canon and into academic study of outlaw, underground, and subcultural forms that span from blues and rap lyrics to performance and slam poetry to slash fiction, the latter produced by fans of many popular TV shows like *Star Trek*.[3] Cultural studies scholars have recently valued such vernacular literary discoveries for what they tell us about social dynamics as well as for their creativity and originality. Parenthetically, film, television, and advertising can be, and have since the 1960s been, studied as literature using methods of literary and cultural analysis. In any case, there is no end in sight, it appears, to the unearthing and appreciation of such marginal and subaltern discourses.

The external changes to American literature, the changes "without," reflect new geographical realities and consciousness. A growing number of contemporary pan-African American writers and scholars, for instance, regard the African diaspora and its literature, particularly as lodged in the expansive Atlantic basin stretching from Britain to Africa to North and South America with the Caribbean included – the so-called Black Atlantic of the slavery trade routes – as a coherent multilingual transnational formation worthy of study.[4] "America," furthermore, has hemispheric connotations. The recent pan-American concept "literatures of the Americas" covers not only multilingual indigenous literature from Alaska to Argentina (Canadian First Nations included), but works in Spanish, French, English, and their dialects from across the region.[5] In addition, some scholars and critics focusing on the literatures of Hawaii have singled out multilingual Polynesian and Asian transnational traditions, spanning across the "American Pacific" from Oceania and Polynesia to the Philippines and Taiwan.[6] Such regional literary formations as the Black Atlantic, the Pacific Basin, and InterAmerican indigenous literature, formed more or less explicitly in the context of globalization, have and will doubtless continue to change the canon of American literature, specifically its geographical reach, its genres, and its languages, displacing the historical Eurocentric core tied to the English language and to the East coast (the Boston–New York–Philadelphia axis).

What have these changes meant for the teaching of American literature? Take, for example, the landmark *Heath Anthology of American Literature*, first published in 1990 and regularly updated since then. The canon continues to be expanded, with substantial coverage of literature by working-class writers, women, African Americans, Hispanics, Native Americans, and Asian Americans, including new genres, revaluations of various existing genres, and coverage of previously taboo themes like child abuse, racial violence, and homosexuality.[7] With the publication in 2000 of the Shell and Sollors *Multilingual Anthology of American Literature*, the English-only foundation of American literature has been not only newly contextualized, but symbolically and officially thrown into question. In addition, American and

127

cultural studies scholars especially have foregrounded the value of "subliterary" genres like romance and science fiction, as well as the importance of regional literatures like those of the Black Atlantic.[8]

From my perspective, as someone who studied American literature during the 1960s, recent changes are astonishing, having the force of a revelation, seeming a liberation. They reflect more broadly the history, scope, and nature of American literary discourse. "Literature" is not restricted, as it was during the mid-twentieth century, to a narrow range of accredited genres and to the purported "best" that has been said and thought based on nowadays highly contested criteria and tastes.[9] Today textbooks and teachers have the opportunity to represent more liberally the literature of the American people. At the same time, however, a great deal of labor, sometimes burdensome, has gone into retrofitting my own knowledge of American literature. This involves not just reading previously ignored material, but reconceptualizing genre and language hierarchies. Many scholars have had to play catchup. More importantly, criteria of merit have had to expand for me and others beyond aesthetic well-madeness, originality in the context of tradition, and intellectual and emotive power to include social and historical representativeness.[10] Theories of literature are not what they used to be.

Over the course of the past four decades, official immigration into the US has been nearly a million people a year on average. The nation is in actual fact, and has long been, multicultural and multilingual. Still, government policies promote English-only melting pot assimilationist ideas and institutions, rather than a more credible rainbow language politics. Not surprisingly, there is a related long-standing politics of American literature scholarship and pedagogy: it pits a homogenizing nationalism and citizen training against heterogeneous traditions and communities divided along lines of race, ethnicity, class, gender, region, religion, and sexuality.[11] Yet national dissensus seems today more multifaceted and wider than ever, and it surfaces more readily in textbooks and classrooms. That to me, as well as others, is a mixed blessing. It involves the complicated narrative of America from the perspective of contemporary multiculturalism, postmodernization, and globalization. I return to these three theoretical topics at the close of the chapter.

British Literature Nowadays

The British literature I studied during the 1960s is very much internally and externally altered today, notably along lines of geography, and less so of language and genre. The official, though grudging, devolution of the United Kingdom in recent decades has highlighted a sense of the separation and separateness from England of Scotland, Ireland, and Wales. Each of these has witnessed renewed interest in their distinct cultural traditions and national languages (Scotch Gaelic, Irish, Welsh). Not incidentally, ethnic revivals and heritage language studies are today commonplace around the post-colonizing world. All this impacts literary studies as well as politics and geography. England itself has its own distinctive regional identities and dialects, with Yorkshire and the southern counties, for example, differentiated from London. Unlike the English–only American literary canon as it existed during the mid-twentieth century, "British literature," as any English major can testify, has a long multilingual history. Old English, Anglo-Norman, Old Norse, Middle English, and Latin textual traditions play various accredited roles. But these dead languages are used mainly for scholarly historical studies of very distant times. Scottish, Irish, and Welsh play minor roles, rejuvenated now and then with revivals, as at the present moment. It was Raymond Williams who noted the narrowing of the concept of literature in England from all books on the library shelf during the eighteenth century to certain meritorious poems, plays, and novels (overwhelmingly written by men and in English) by the mid-twentieth century.[12] Not surprisingly, the recent expansion of the British canon has incorporated formerly excluded popular genres like science and mystery fiction. And it has redignified such genres as letters, travel writing, diaries, conduct books, sermons, and ballads (the latter two being oral genres). Also it has acknowledged new

129

forms like chants and dub. Just as British literature nowadays covers a wider range of forms and languages and dialects, it includes yet further transformations and expansions due to postwar immigration and decolonization.

Since World War Two, waves of immigrants from the West Indies, South Asia, the Middle East, and Africa have increasingly rendered England a less homogeneous, more multicultural country. This is reflected in its contemporary literature, which, however, remains steadfastly monolingual, with other languages, dialects, creoles, and pidgins positioned as fringe elements. In addition, the longstanding British Commonwealth of Nations, simultaneously attenuated yet still in place and even expanded to include 50 nations in recent decades, accords the English-language literature of, for example, Australia, Canada, New Zealand, South Africa, and many other nations the uncertain status of "British" (more or less). And "Black British" literature, consisting of works by South Asian as well as African and West Indian authors residing in England, constitutes by now a widely recognized category.[13] So among British writers today are Chinua Achebe (Nigeria), J. M. Coetzee (South Africa), Nadine Gordimer (South Africa), V. S. Naipaul (Trinidad), Ngugi wa Thiongo (Kenya), Michael Ondaatje (Sri Lanka), Salman Rushdie (India), and Derek Walcott (St Lucia). These are all problem cases by earlier standards and no doubt still arguable today in various quarters.

Like the parallel categories Francophone, Hispanophone, Luso-phone, and Sinophone, Anglophone literature covers all the literatures in English globally considered. This classification came into its own in recent decades and remains a work in progress. Among the key theoretical questions it raises are what counts as literature and as English? For instance, would an English-language African ritual drama with some regional pidgin and with music, dance, and costume be Anglophone literature? How about works in other distinctive English dialects, creoles, patois, indigenous forms?[14] A creation of the contemporary global era, Anglophone literature is transnational, multiracial, multicultural. It is in large part a legacy of British expansion, colonization, and recent decolonization, but dating back many centuries and not simply a contemporary phenomenon. On one hand, the Anglophone world subsumes regional formations like the Black Atlantic and Pacific Basin. On the other hand, this large-scale global form co-occurs with and does not threaten such distinctive transnational regional formations. Local and global coexist, as the slogan has it; often the global heightens the local while the local rewrites the global.[15]

What have all these changes meant for the teaching of British literature? When we look at a pioneering textbook like the *Arnold Anthology of Post-colonial Literatures in English*, published in 1996, we find Anglophone literature spreading out from the United Kingdom and the US to Africa, Australia, Canada, the Caribbean, New Zealand, the South Pacific, and South and Southeast Asia. A final section of the book is devoted to "trans-cultural writing": it acknowledges the "impossibility of confining migrant writing within the strait-jacket of national or regional labels."[16] Among its noncanonical genres are an Acoli song of abuse, drum chants, radio play, and family album. Indigenous writers are included. As I write, British literature in many places is gradually being transformed into "Literatures in English," a category recognized more and more by higher education departments of English. Whether focused on England, the United Kingdom, the Anglophone World, or all three, British literature is nowadays a hodgepodge of genres, languages, traditions – potentially. No doubt, a "Multilingual Anthology of British Literature" should exist by now (if it doesn't already). It should cover not only the past, but the heteroglot present as well.

Much recent scholarship on British literature is more resolutely historical, multicultural, and globally oriented than during the 1960s heyday of formalism. Its teaching and textbooks include more women and immigrant and minority writers, plus a wider array of genres, some formerly set on the fringes or excluded from the canon. Interestingly, the great writers, such as Chaucer, Shakespeare, and Milton, receive as much prominence and attention as previously. However, new contemporary critical concerns and theoretical questions have been more insistently put to their works, which has happened to all literary works since the 1960s.

131

Here is a typical set of postformalist critical questions put to literature nowadays. What role does gender play? How do distinctions of social class operate? Are racial hierarchies in play? What kinds of social regulations, norms, and deviances are present and permitted? Do social and political resistances or subversions circulate in the works? Do transnational genres, themes, and characters, European and otherwise, operate? What are the impacts of trade and travel? Who had and has access to these works? How were they produced and distributed, both technically and politically as well as economically speaking? What modes of literary ownership pertain? These questions were not regularly asked when I was a student during the 1960s. Literary studies is not what it used to be.

Widely respected concerns and questions, of course, survive from the early postwar formalist days of being an English major. Here is a set of characteristic formalist critical questions addressed to literature then and now. What motivates character? How does the author structure the work? Are there elements of language, imagery, and style, especially original features of style, meriting attention? What role does genre play? How does the individual work relate to the author's oeuvre and to literary tradition? Are there cruxes or problems with the textual reliability of the work? Do any elements of biography or critical legacy contribute to interpreting individual texts? My own experience is that these questions and concerns from an earlier era play minor roles in the academic study of British as well as American literature and theory nowadays.

In light of the expansion of courses, modules, and texts covering women's literature, the literatures of minorities, popular and pulp literature,[17] plus postcolonial and Anglophone literature, the study of major canonical figures like Shakespeare occupies more of a separate niche today. The mainstream of British literature has been segmented into sets of numerous tributaries. That positions the "greats" at once as still a bit above the ordinary flows, but paradoxically as part of the general discourse of culture open to criticism and not sacrosanct. Given the spread of popular culture and new media during recent decades, a gradual sense of the antiquation of canonical literature has manifested itself among increasing numbers of students. Nowadays Chaucer and Milton appear to loom less dominantly, while courses devoted to them feel more specialized. For his part, Shakespeare seems more rooted in the popular culture of his time and ours as well. This is thanks to the richness of his work, to new historicist scholarship, and to ceaseless productions particularly on television and film. While the idea of the genius author survives, this figures today represents and speaks of and for his or her times, seeming less transcendent than a generation ago. Bogus, often rightist tracts aside, the major writer today occupies an important, though somewhat diminished space in the culture and the curriculum.

Canons, Postmodernization, Globalization, Multiculturalism

In the US university, as elsewhere, the infrastructure of literary studies over the past century has depended on the categories of nation, historical period, genre, and major figure. Students, faculty, courses, and textbooks study and specialize in, for example, nineteenth-century American poetry, seventeenth-century English drama, Shakespeare (Early or Late Works), Modern British and American fiction, and so on. The same is true of both foreign and comparative literary studies where scholars examine and teach such areas as the nineteenth-century French novel, twentieth-century Italian drama, the works of Goethe, or Comparative Romantic Poetry (English, French, German).[18] Nation, period, genre, major figure – that is overwhelmingly the model. How have recent events transformed things?

On one hand, a great deal has changed, but on the other very little seems altered in today's literary studies from what it was a generation ago. English majors today, to illustrate change, generally have some contact with the more or less separate spheres of ethnic and women's literatures, Black Atlantic and Anglophone postcolonial writers, and popular and subcultural genres. This is quite different from four decades ago. But, of course, none of it is multilingual, remaining

133

English-only, with some increased exposure to "dialects." The required courses for the major follow the old tried-and-true paradigm: one or two methods and theory courses, one major writer course, two surveys of literature, plus four or five period courses, usually spread across several genres. So the matrix of nation–period–genre–major writer remains in place. Recent changes are added on in the form of optional or elective courses as well as adjustments, invariably inclusions, to existing courses such as surveys of English or American literature, eighteenth-century fiction, nineteenth-century American novel, modern British poetry, medieval literature, contemporary US drama, etc. Academic departments and programs for majors change slowly and grudgingly. When change comes, it typically takes the form of addition, not transformation, preferring a nonthreatening cafeteria approach. But enough supplementing constitutes transformation, which, in retrospect, is how things now stand. Allow me to elaborate, focusing on the literary canon as an example.

The canonical genres of Western academic literary study are and continue to be poetry, drama, and fiction. This matrix is attended by a finely calibrated chart from late Renaissance times of central and peripheral genres and subgenres. In the realm of poetry, for instance, the epic remains a major genre; romance epic slightly less major; the substantial sonnet sequence less major still; the individual sonnet minor; the epigram very minor; the limerick subliterary. With the addition and legitimation of new literary genres in recent decades, various incommensurable things have happened to the canon. It has been expanded obviously. Yet the hierarchy of canonical genres, though widely challenged, is still in place, notably in curricula and in the professional unconscious of faculty. Significantly, the canon has also been adroitly sidestepped and rendered beside the point. This would (or might) be the case especially in studies of contemporary material, for instance, science fiction, postwar popular poetry, contemporary African American drama, women's pulp fiction, or Anglophone mystery fiction. So the recent proliferation of literatures and genres has expanded, repositioned, and flexibilized the canon.

In some circumstances it has been expanded and democratized. In others it has been sidestepped; in yet others, it has been productively mimicked, particularly in the creation of anthologies of new literatures. In still others, it has more or less maintained its century-old standing.[19] This is a case of uneven development, a frequently attested feature of postmodern culture.[20]

The many changes recorded thus far add up to and reflect the postmodernization of literary study. By postmodern I mean what Fredric Jameson, David Harvey, and many other cultural critics do, namely the distinct late twentieth- and early twenty-first-century period of culture characterized as postindustrial (or third-stage capitalist), exhibiting a wide array of distinctive features. Here I recite a dozen such widely attested relevant traits: the divide between high and low cultures weakens; the modern autonomy of spheres erodes; crises of representation occur; new social movements (notably women's and civil rights ones) displace traditional political parties as innovative forces; societies become explicitly, sometimes officially, multicultural; big government, big labor, and big business get downsized (unevenly to be sure); the human subject becomes a decentered posthuman cyborg, occupying multiple subject positions; the multiversity replaces the college; new disciplines like women's, ethnic, postcolonial, and cultural studies arise; and grand narratives undergo deconstruction. Nowadays common among literary and cultural critics, a whole array of contemporary buzz words usefully signal postmodernization: for example, difference, micropolitics, heterogeneity, rainbow coalitions, interpretive communities, heteroglossia, multiculturalism, hybridization, intertextuality, vernacular theory, interdisciplinarity, fusion, pastiche. What most characterizes postmodernity, I have shown in *Living with Theory* and elsewhere, is disorganization or, more descriptively, disaggregation.[21] This is what has happened more or less to American and British literatures and, in general, to literary and cultural studies since the 1960s: proliferation of distinct elements, new forms and assemblages, dehierarchizations, tolerance for incommensurabilities and differences, multiplication of perspectives, adding up to postmodern transformation.

135

In what way does the much-discussed phenomenon of globalization operate in this scenario? While it has been going on since the European explorations and colonizations during the early Renaissance, if not before, globalization entered a new phase starting in the latter part of the twentieth century. This is symbolized by the spread of nuclear power, space missions, global warming, and floating currencies. One other very significant hallmark is the growth of transnational organizations like the United Nations, World Bank, International Monetary Fund, World Trade Organization, and multinational corporations. Such institutions facilitate increased worldwide flows of money, goods, services, people, and information. They promote laissez-faire economics and multiculturalism (official and happenstance), plus cultural fusions and cosmopolitanism.[22]

No sketch of the phenomenon of globalization can omit mention of the many disparate reactions to or accompanying it. These range from movements for decolonization, local autonomy, and indigenous rights to environmentalism, diasporic unity, and collectively recovered memory to protective barriers, calls for economic redistribution, and renationalizations (as in the USSR). All these phenomena fit today under the cover term "globalization." The World Social Forum serves as a productive venue for many of the antiglobalization forces. Globalization in this context is often negatively equated with a whole array of phenomena such as aggressive Westernization, Americanization, modernization, colonialism, imperialism, empire, hegemony, neoliberal capitalism, rampant commodification, homogenization. Finally, globalization is sometimes cast as a questionable grand narrative, a performative, a myth, a fantasy.[23]

So while globalization has its champions, its critics, and its skeptics, it serves in my argument, as the chapter title suggests, to portray metaphorically the recent postmodern transformations of American and British literatures. This entails internal changes like the emergence of ethnic and minority literatures and their distinct genres, as well as external changes such as the upsurge of transnational forms like indigenous, transatlantic, and Anglophone literatures. Here as elsewhere, globalization raises many questions for criticism and theory not only about fusions, multiculturalism, cosmopolitanism, and diasporas, but also about identity politics, separatist autonomy, decolonization, and multilingualism.[24]

To the extent that the contemporary keyword globalization designates homogenized global English and hegemonic Anglophone literature, it represents a central, often rightly lamented and criticized part of the postmodern experience. But that flat definition downplays the coming to voice of suppressed minorities, subalterns, forgotten others in minor and major languages and forms. It should not. American and British literatures and the English major do risk being unreflective parts of the project of neoliberal globalization. In this event, literary study serves as an instrument of imperial power. However, by its *critical* handling and reception, potentially resistant, ironic, humorous, angry, it can be turned against any simple one-way hegemonic mission.[25] Exchange has the word change in it. The ability to read critically against the grain and to say no in thunder, laughter, or whatever skeptical register, can make a difference. It is possible to bear witness against the concentrated wealth, influence, power, and knowledge of dominant interests. Moral and political stakes are, as always, at issue in the study of literature, the curriculum, the canon, theory and criticism.[26]

Beneath the managed official multiculturalism of recently expanded and postmodernized British and American literary canons, there lies the possibility of further radicalizations of a critical multiculturalism. This could reach beyond the formal legal equality of each nowadays characteristically monolingual English-speaking national subject, who is positioned as a free agent, living and acting in a Darwinian world of vicious competition, to an ecologically aware and engaged citizen-subject open to heteroglot social worlds and languages, encouraged in cooperation, doubtless nationalistic but not blindly so, committed to economic as well as social justice at home and abroad, all the while retaining rights to autonomy, difference, criticism, freedom from and of religion. One way to temper the happy faux multiculturalism of consensus – the kind of thing displayed in the US by the mariachi and steel bands followed by

Native American dancers at the ubiquitous local festivals sponsored by corporations and chambers of commerce[27] – is to argue that we human beings are all gendered, class-identified, and ethnic, not just privately but publicly and plurally so. There should be, in any case, no colorless homogeneous, yet hierarchical, dominant unmarked core of the social order, masked and privileged and tolerant of others. Despite controversy, such critical multiculturalism represents an essential contribution from contemporary theory to conceptions of identity, politics, literature, and culture. No defense, no manifesto committed to living with the significant contributions of theory can fail today to foster a critical multiculturalism fitted to our increasingly globalized and postmodernized world. This is a space where theory, politics, and literature intersect in potentially life-enhancing ways.

Notes

Chapter 1   Theory Ends

An early version of this chapter was published in *Profession 2005* (New York: Modern Language Association, 2005).

1   See, for example, Allan Bloom's famous early complaint against theory, *The Closing of the American Mind* (New York: Simon & Schuster, 1987), and John M. Ellis's later lament, *Literature Lost: Social Agendas and the Corruption of the Humanities* (New Haven: Yale University Press, 1997).

2   See the landmark neopragmatist text by Steven Knapp and Walter Benn Michaels, "Against Theory," in W. J. T. Mitchell, ed., *Against Theory: Literary Studies and the New Pragmatism* (Chicago: University of Chicago Press, 1985), pp. 11–30, and the many latter-day works of Stanley Fish that programmatically renounce theory, as, for example, "Dennis Martinez and the Uses of Theory," in *Doing What Comes Naturally* (Durham: Duke University Press, 1989), pp. 372–98.

3   In addition to the well-known hermeneutical work of E. D. Hirsch, Jr, see, for instance, Wendell V. Harris, *Literary Meaning: Reclaiming the Study of Literature* (New York: New York University Press, 1996), and Satya P. Mohanty, *Literary Theory and the Claims of History: Postmodernism, Objectivity, Multicultural Politics* (Ithaca: Cornell University Press, 1997).

4   Jeffrey Williams, "The Posttheory Generation," in Peter C. Herman, ed., *Day Late, Dollar Short: The Next Generation and the New Academy* (Albany: State University of New York Press, 2000), pp. 25–43.

5   See, for example, Edward W. Said, "The Problem of Textuality: Two Exemplary Positions," *Critical Inquiry* 4.4 (Summer 1978): 673–714; Robert Scholes, *Textual Power: Literary Theory and the Teaching of English* (New Haven: Yale University Press, 1985), esp. chs 5 and 6; Barbara Christian, "The Race for Theory," *Cultural Critique* 6 (Spring 1987): 51–63; and Sandra M. Gilbert and Susan Gubar, "The Mirror and the Vamp: Reflections on Feminist Criticism," in Ralph Cohen, ed., *The Future of Literary Theory* (New York: Routledge, 1989), pp. 144–66.

See also David Gorman, "Theory, Antitheory, and Countertheory," *Philosophy and Literature* 21.2 (1997): 455–65, which helpfully distinguishes three modes of antitheory from "countertheory." The latter is a movement skeptical and critical of poststructuralism and amenable to alternatives such as hermeneutics and speech-act theory. Note that for Gorman the root "theory" means poststructuralism. Also see Daphne Patai and Will H. Corral, eds, *Theory's Empire: An Anthology of Dissent* (New York: Columbia University Press, 2005), which gathers four dozen anti- and countertheory statements.

6   According to Jonathan Culler, in *On Deconstruction: Theory and Criticism after Structuralism* (Ithaca: Cornell University Press, 1982), today "works of literary theory are closely and vitally related to other writings within a domain as yet unnamed but often called 'theory' for short.... Many of its most interesting works do not explicitly address literature. It is not 'philosophy' in the current sense of the term, since it includes Saussure, Marx, Freud, Erving Goffman, and Jacques Lacan as well as Hegel, Nietzsche, and Hans–Georg Gadamer.... This new genre is certainly heterogeneous" (p. 8). Fredric Jameson similarly notes, in his "Postmodernism and Consumer Society," in E. Ann Kaplan, ed., *Postmodernism and Its Discontents: Theories, Practices* (New York: Verso, 1988): "A generation ago there was still a technical discourse of professional philosophy ... alongside which one could still distinguish that quite different discourse of the other academic disciplines – of political science, for example, or sociology or literary criticism. Today, increasingly, we have a kind of writing simply called 'theory' which is all or none of those things at once" (p. 14). Recently, Jonathan Culler, in *The Literary in Theory* (Stanford: Stanford University Press, 2007), observed: "Theory has triumphed in that it is everywhere these days..." (p. 256). Moreover, "we are inexorably in theory, whether we champion or deplore it" (p. 96).

Insofar as both contemporary theory and postmodernism are often linked with social constructivism, standpoint epistemology, cultural relativism, and popular culture (versus the literary canon), they constitute threats and often targets for conservative thinkers, left- and right-wing.

7   For various perspectives, see Martin McQuillan et al., eds, *Post-theory: New Directions in Criticism* (Edinburgh: Edinburgh University Press, 1999); Judith Butler, John Guillory, and Kendall Thomas, eds, *What's Left of Theory?* (New York: Routledge, 2000); Michael Payne and John Schad, eds, *Life. After. Theory* (London: Continuum, 2003); Terry Eagleton, *After Theory* (New York: Basic, 2003); and Jennifer Howard, "The Fragmentation of Literary Theory," *Chronicle of Higher Education*, 16 Dec. 2005, A12–16. See also Terry Eagleton, *The Function of Criticism: The Spectator to Post-Structuralism* (London: Verso, 1984), which provides an assessment of the changing roles of criticism and theory in modern capitalist society from the 1720s to the 1980s.

8   On the situation of the higher education sector of the economy, see chapter 6, "The Politics of Academic Labor," which surveys many sources on the topic.
9   Globalization today has also meant the devolution of national literatures toward loose assemblages composed of different regions, languages, and ethnic and minority groups. Not surprisingly, the number of recognized genres has increased and the hierarchy has changed, expanding the definition of literature. For the example of US literature, see both Paul Lauter, gen. ed., *The Heath Anthology of American Literature*, 5th edn (Boston: Houghton Mifflin, 2004), and Marc Shell and Werner Sollors, eds, *The Multilingual Anthology of American Literature* (New York: New York University Press, 2000). Shell and Sollors provide original texts and translations from 20 languages, ranging from Lenape, Massachusett, Navajo, French, Spanish, and Arabic to Chinese, German, Italian, Polish, Welsh, and Yiddish. A full discussion is offered in chapter 8 below, "Globalization of Literatures."

Chapter 2   Teaching Theory Now

1   David Horowitz, *The Professors: The 101 Most Dangerous Academics in America* (Washington, DC: Regnery, 2006), p. xxv. Among "dangerous" American theorists malevolently caricatured in Horowitz's 101 profiles are Stanley Aronowitz, Amiri Baraka, Michael Bérubé, Noam Chomsky, bell hooks, Fredric Jameson, Eve Kosovsky Sedgwick, and Michael Warner. The last of many alarmist, wildly exaggerated sentences in this book reads "the problems revealed in this text – the explicit introduction of political agendas into the classroom, the lack of professionalism in conduct, and the decline in professional standards – appear to be increasingly widespread throughout the academic profession and at virtually every type of institution of higher learning" (p. 377).
2   Gerald Graff, *Beyond the Culture Wars: How Teaching the Conflicts Can Revitalize American Education* (New York: Norton, 1990). On critical pedagogy, see my "Postmodernism, Pedagogy, and Cultural Criticism," in Vincent B. Leitch, *Postmodernism – Local Effects, Global Flows* (Albany: State University of New York Press, 1996), ch. 11, which critically examines Stanley Aronowitz and Henry Giroux's *Postmodern Education: Politics, Culture, and Social Criticism* (Minneapolis: University of Minnesota Press, 1991). See also Antonia Darder, Marta Baltodano, and Rodolfo D. Torres, eds, *The Critical Pedagogy Reader* (New York: RoutledgeFalmer, 2003).
3   Richard Ohmann, *English in America: A Radical View of the Profession* (New York: Oxford University Press, 1976); and Pierre Bourdieu and Jean-Claude Passeron, *Reproduction in Education, Society and Culture*, trans. Richard Nice (1970; London: Sage, 1977).

4   See the pioneering "MLA Survey Casts Light on Canon Debate," *MLA Newsletter* 23.4 (Winter 1991): 12–14, which concludes "for many literature teachers there is no contradiction between wishing students to appreciate Western tradition and wishing them to be aware of the influence of race, class, and gender on the creation and dissemination of literary texts" (p. 13); and also Bettina J. Huber, "Today's Literature Classroom: Findings from the MLA's 1990 Survey of Upper-Division Courses," *Association of Departments of English Bulletin*, 101 (Spring 1992): 36–60, an exhaustive study that concludes: "The findings reported thus far provide no evidence that English faculty members have abandoned traditional texts in upper-division literature courses" (p. 43). Furthermore, "Although recent literary criticism is included among the required readings for many upper-division literature courses, its role is small" (p. 45). These findings still hold today.

5   Northrop Frye, *Anatomy of Criticism: Four Essays* (Princeton: Princeton University Press, 1957): "The difficulty often felt in 'teaching literature' arises from the fact that it cannot be done: the criticism of literature is all that can be directly taught" (p. 11).

6   Robert Scholes, *Textual Power: Literary Theory and the Teaching of English* (New Haven: Yale University Press, 1985), esp. ch. 2: "My point here is that criticism is always made on behalf of a group" (p. 24).

7   Gerald Graff, "Advocacy in the Classroom – Or the Curriculum? A Response," in Patricia Meyer Spacks, ed., *Advocacy in the Classroom: Problems and Possibilities* (New York: St Martin's Press, 1996). This book collects 37 papers and two responses from a 1995 conference sponsored by 16 scholarly organizations in the midst of the culture wars. In his response Graff concludes, "If any consensus emerges from the chapters in this volume, it is Advocacy, Yes, Indoctrination, No" (p. 427). In addition, he observes "many of the most acclaimed teachers since Plato have possessed a streak of fanaticism and inflexibility" (p. 428).

8   Vincent B. Leitch and Mitchell R. Lewis, "Cultural Studies," in Michael Groden, Martin Kreiswirth, and Imre Szeman, eds, *Johns Hopkins Guide to Literary Theory and Criticism*, 2nd edn (Baltimore: Johns Hopkins University Press, 2005), pp. 224–30.

9   See Vincent B. Leitch et al. (eds), *Norton Anthology of Theory and Criticism* (New York: Norton, 2001); and also M. Keith Booker, *Teaching with the Norton Anthology of Theory and Criticism: A Guidebook for Instructors* (New York: Norton, 2001); plus Dianne F. Sadoff and William Cain, eds, *Teaching Contemporary Theory to Undergraduates* (New York: Modern Language Association, 1994).

10   See, for instance, Jean-Michel Rabaté, *The Future of Theory* (Malden: Blackwell, 2002), which a bit grudgingly concludes with an admittedly subjective list of ten growth areas shaping theory's future (pp. 146–8): material culture, technoscience, globalization studies, ethical criticism, trauma studies, new textual

bibliography, chaos theory, late deconstructive hauntology, new wave ethnic studies, and translation studies. See also Terry Eagleton, *After Theory* (New York: Basic, 2003), where, while noting the passing of the "golden age of cultural theory" (1965–80), he declares: "Those to whom the title of this book suggests that 'theory' is now over, and that we can all relievedly return to an age of pre-theoretical innocence, are in for a disappointment. There can be no going back . . . " (p. 1).

Chapter 3 Applied Theory

1   "Disorganization" depicts the disaggregations, positive and negative, characteristic of contemporary free-market neoliberal economics and society, such as corporate restructuring, subcontracting, deregulation, privatization, conglomeration, temporary contracts, fast turnovers, and ubiquitous labor flexibilizations. See Scott Lash and John Urry, *The End of Organized Capitalism* (Madison: University of Wisconsin Press, 1987); David Harvey, *The Condition of Postmodernity* (Cambridge: Blackwell, 1990); and Tom Peters, *Liberation Management: Necessary Disorganization for the Nanosecond Nineties* (New York: Knopf, 1992). Harvey observes: "For what is most interesting about the current situation is the way in which capitalism is becoming ever more tightly organized *through* dispersal, geographical mobility, and flexible responses in labour markets, labour processes, and consumer markets . . . " (p. 159).

2   For the history of recent contending literary theories of reading, see my *American Literary Criticism from the 1930s to the 1980s* (New York: Columbia University Press, 1988), and also my *Theory Matters* (New York: Routledge, 2003), ch. 1, a critical synopsis and critique of formalist, deconstructive, and cultural studies reading protocols. For a broad survey of trends in reader-response criticism and theory, see Patrocinio P. Schweickart and Elizabeth A. Flynn, eds, *Reading Sites: Social Difference and Reader Response* (New York: Modern Language Association, 2004). This is a follow-up collection to the often-cited predecessor, Elizabeth A. Flynn and Patrocinio P. Schweickart, eds, *Gender and Reading: Essays on Readers, Texts, and Contexts*. (Baltimore: Johns Hopkins University Press, 1986).

3   Stanley E. Fish, *Is There a Text in This Class? The Authority of Interpretive Communities* (Cambridge: Harvard University Press, 1980).

4   Janice A. Radway, *Reading the Romance: Women, Patriarchy, and Popular Literature* (1984; Chapel Hill: University of North Carolina Press, 1991), with new introduction (1991), p. 196.

5   In a slightly later article, "Reception Study: Ethnography and the Problems of Dispersed Audiences and Nomadic Subjects," *Cultural Studies* 2.3 (1988), Radway notes "in my own analysis of a small group of romance readers there is no discussion whatsoever of the ways in which the practice of romance reading

143

might be articulated with practices organized by and centering on race or class" (p. 367). See also the later retrospective "Culture of Reading: An Interview with Janice Radway," *Minnesota Review* 65–6 (2006): 133–48.

6   Henry Jenkins, *Textual Poachers: Television Fans and Participatory Culture* (New York: Routledge, 1992), pp. 26–7. The celebrated idea of reading as poaching that refunctions materials and improvises tactics comes from Michel de Certeau, *The Practice of Everyday Life*, trans. Steven Rendall (Berkeley: University of California Press, 1984), ch. 12. For a later account of Jenkins's more fully articulated theoretical position, see the editors' "A Manifesto for a New Cultural Studies," in Henry Jenkins, Tara McPherson, and Jane Shattuc, eds, *Hop on Pop: The Politics and Pleasures of Popular Culture* (Durham: Duke University Press, 2002), pp. 3–26.

7   On the dynamics and history of rereading, see Matei Calinescu, *Rereading* (New Haven: Yale University Press, 1993), esp. chs 6 and 17 that discuss the intensive (versus extensive) reading of scripture.

8   Thomas McLaughlin, *Street Smarts and Critical Theory: Listening to the Vernacular* (Madison: University of Wisconsin Press, 1996), p. 159.

9   See, for example, Roger Chartier's broad survey of changing reading practices from 1500 to 1800 in his misleadingly titled "The Practical Impact of Writing," in Roger Chartier, ed., *Passions of the Renaissance*, trans. Arthur Goldhammer (Cambridge: Harvard University Press, 1989), pp. 111–59 – which is volume 3 of Philippe Ariès and Georges Duby, gen. eds, *A History of Private Life*. In this chapter Chartier historicizes early modern modes of reading, notably reading aloud, reading alone and in groups, and reading silently and privately. See also George Steiner, "The End of Bookishness?" *Times Literary Supplement*, July 8–14, 1988, p. 754, which glumly portrays postmodernity's antiquation of the critical reading of books as part of the closing down of modernity here dating from the Renaissance: "I would not be surprised if that which lies ahead for classical modes of reading resembles the monasticism from which those modes sprung."

10 Michael Warner, "Uncritical Reading," in Jane Gallop, ed., *Polemic: Critical or Uncritical*, Essays from the English Institute (New York: Routledge, 2004), p. 15.

11 The term vernacular during postmodern times and within cultural studies circles, as used, for example, in common phrases like vernacular reading, vernacular art, vernacular theory, designates derivation from the people, the community, the region or locale. It is contrasted explicitly against the establishment, the hegemonic order, the official. Vernacular typically connotes unschooled, nonacademic, outsider art and language linked by implication with participatory, noncommodified ways of life. Its widespread use among contemporary academics reflects the shift of focus from canonical to popular culture. It bears witness to the breaching of the high/low cultural divide characteristic of postmodern culture and the field of cultural studies (itself a new postmodern discipline). Additionally, the term vernacular is connected to

144

the mission and survival of the humanities as well as to many contemporary backlashes. The latter are usually mounted by conservatives against academic scholarly preoccupation with forms of vernacular versus canonical culture. Such vernacular forms range from pulp fiction (romance, horror, sci-fi), ethnic arts, television, and Hollywood movies to rock music, youth subcultures, zines, etc. In this political context, vernacular is not a neutral term.

12   On postmodernity see my *Postmodernism – Local Effects, Global Flows* (Albany: State University of New York Press, 1996). See also the reader–response reader, James L. Machor and Philip Goldstein, eds, *Reception Study: From Literary Theory to Cultural Studies* (New York: Routledge, 2001), which hints at a similar broad historical framework for reading in its promotion of receptionist over formalist study: "Both modern and postmodern reception study defend the historical against the purely formal approach, undertake the historical study of a text's diverse readings, and repudiate the autonomous norms and values of traditional theory; however, postmodern reception study also adopts the poststructuralist critique of 'foundational' theory. Moreover, more fully than modern reception study, postmodern reception study examines women's, African-American, and multicultural literatures, popular culture, the ordinary reader, the history of the book, and so on" (p. xiii). This text contains selections from Fish, Radway, and more than a dozen other scholars; it includes a lengthy selected bibliography on reception studies (pp. 345–88).

13   See Mary Ann Caws, ed., *Textual Analysis: Some Readers Reading* (New York: Modern Language Association, 1986), which self-consciously registers the pluralization of venerable close reading with two dozen variegated samples, five of which present deconstructors going in different directions. Note that the deconstructive phenomena of misreading and of the so-called unreadability of texts systematically beget redoubled exegesis. Among those contemporary scholars who most admire rigorous close reading are deconstructors. For a discussion of different modes of deconstructive close reading, see my *Deconstructive Criticism* (New York: Columbia University Press, 1983), which includes but goes beyond the usual de Man versus Derrida analysis of reading protocols and strategies.

Chapter 4   Theory Fusions

1   See www.neh.gov and www.nhalliance.org.
2   See Alvin Kernan, *What's Happened to the Humanities?* (Princeton: Princeton University Press, 1997), which offers selections from two conferences on the state of the humanities supported by the Andrew W. Mellon Foundation and which provides 16 statistical tables and figures documenting decline: "The

humanities, in plain words, have become a less and less significant part of higher education" (p. 6). See also Jennifer Howard, "Reading and Writing Get Arithmetic," *Chronicle of Higher Education*, April 14, 2006, which reports that a consortium of major humanities organizations, funded by the American Academy of Arts and Sciences and the Andrew W. Mellon Foundation, initiated in 2005 a long-term data-collecting project, "Humanities Indicators," to update Kernan's data. Their model is the US National Science Foundation's influential biennial "Science and Engineering Indicators."

3 See, for example, Robert Scholes, "Presidential Address 2004: The Humanities in a Posthumanist World," *PMLA* 120.3 (May 2005): 724–33, and Jacques Derrida, "The University without Condition," in *Without Alibi*, ed. and trans. Peggy Kamuf (Stanford: Stanford University Press, 2002), pp. 202–37. Derrida here offers a vigorous defense of academic humanities.

4 See, for example, Julie Thompson Klein, *Humanities, Culture, and Interdisciplinarity: The Changing American Academy* (Albany: State University of New York Press, 2005), which also provides a bibliography (pp. 221–49).

5 See the wide-ranging review essay by Jeffrey J. Williams, "The Post-Welfare State University," *American Literary History* 18 (Spring 2006): 190–216.

Chapter 5   Late Derrida

Written a few weeks before Derrida's death, this chapter appeared in a special memorial issue on Derrida of *Critical Inquiry* 33.2 (Winter 2007).

1 A comprehensive bibliographical source can be found online in Peter Krapp, "Bibliography of Publications by Jacques Derrida," at www.hydra.umn.edu/derrida/jdind.html.

2 Jacques Derrida and Maurizio Ferraris, *A Taste for the Secret*, ed. G. Donis and David Webb, trans. Giacomo Donis (1997; Cambridge: Polity, 2001), p. 62. This book contains five dialogues of Ferraris and Derrida between July 1993 and November 1994, plus one of Gianni Vattimo and Derrida in January 1995. "Starting in the 1990s, Derrida's tendency to write in outline became even more pronounced as he delivered bits and pieces of [for example] a thesis on hospitality that one had to glean from a number of different texts" – Herman Rapaport, *Later Derrida: Reading the Recent Work* (New York: Routledge, 2003), p. 26. Rapaport's book focuses on a range of topics, though not politics.

3 Geoffrey Bennington and Jacques Derrida, *Jacques Derrida*, rev. edn, trans. G. Bennington (Chicago: University of Chicago Press, 1999), p. 169; and Nicholas Royle, *Jacques Derrida* (London: Routledge, 2003), p. 96. In a documentary,

Derrida is quoted from an unpublished 1982 interview that sets improvisation against stereotypical discourse, revealing "I believe in improvisation" – *Derrida*, dir. Kirby Dick and Amy Ziering Kofman, Jane Doe Films, 2002; DVD, Zeitgeist Video, 2003, ch. 10.

4   Jacques Derrida, *Voyous* (Rogues) (Paris: Galilée, 2003), p. 12. My translation. Hereafter all translations from this text are mine.

5   In "Derrida and Politics," Geoffrey Bennington notes "There is no easy way to distinguish logical concerns from epistemological ones in Derrida, nor these from ethical or political ones" – in Tom Cohen, ed., *Jacques Derrida and the Humanities: A Critical Reader* (Cambridge: Cambridge University Press, 2001), p. 197. In *Derrida & the Political* (London: Routledge, 1996), Richard Beardsworth observes "the domain of politics is not a privileged object of reflection for Derrida, although recent work of the 1990s has mobilized and reworked the term more immediately than that of the past" (p. xi). In his otherwise excellent *Ethics – Politics – Subjectivity: Essays on Derrida, Levinas and Contemporary French Thought* (London: Verso, 1999), Simon Critchley unconvincingly declares "in my experience of reading Derrida, the closer one looks, the harder it is to find any substantial difference between earlier and later work " (p. 96). On the contrary, the later work appears both more haphazard and more preoccupied with politics and ethics. In his *Derrida, Responsibility and Politics* (Aldershot: Ashgate, 1997), Morag Patrick defends Derrida against charges of ethicopolitical nihilism, and in the process he reviews many political criticisms launched against Derrida during his career. However, nothing is said about sovereignty, a key concern of Derrida's late work. Preliminary observations on the politics of sovereignty appear in Seyla Benhabib, "Democracy and Difference: Reflections on the Metapolitics of Lyotard and Derrida" (1994), reprinted in Christopher Norris and David Roden, eds, *Jacques Derrida* (London: Sage, 2003), vol. 4, esp. pp. 221–8. Part of the series Sage Masters of Modern Thought, this four-volume work reprints 65 articles and book chapters of critical reaction to Derrida dating from the 1970s into the new century. Despite its 1,600 pages and 22 topics, the critical legacy is highly selective, privileging philosophers and philosophy.

6   Jacques Derrida and Elisabeth Roudinesco, *De quoi demain . . . Dialogue* (For What Tomorrow . . . A Dialogue) (Paris: Flammarion, 2001), p. 151. My translation. Hereafter all translations from this text are mine.

7   Jacques Derrida, *Without Alibi*, ed. and trans. Peggy Kamuf (Stanford: Stanford University Press, 2002), p. 268. This book contains five late addresses and essays plus a foreword by Derrida. Kamuf observes "what is perhaps the book's essential trait, common to all its chapters: the trait of sovereignty" (p. xiii). For a useful discussion of Derrida's thinking on violence, see David C. Durst, "The Place of the Political in Derrida and Foucault," *Political Theory* 28.5 (Oct. 2000): 675–89, which is a review essay of Beardsworth's *Derrida & the Political* and Jon Simon's *Foucault & the Political* (London: Routledge, 1995).

8   Jacques Derrida, *Negotiations: Interventions and Interviews, 1971–2001*, ed. and trans. Elizabeth Rottenberg (Stanford: Stanford University Press, 2002), p. 385. This extensive collection, notes the dust jacket, "encompasses the political and ethical thinking of Jacques Derrida over thirty years."

   Among the most paradoxical features of sovereignty are the dynamics of time and language. The essential "indivisibility" of sovereignty is undermined by temporality and history as well as by discourse's soliciting of the other and its dividing of authority (*Voyous*, p. 144). Derrida does not follow up on these provocative disruptions.

   Here is another vexing trait of sovereignty: "The sovereign has the right not to respond; he has a right to the silence of this asymmetry. He has a right to a certain irresponsibility" – Jacques Derrida, "La bête et le souverain" (The Beast and the Sovereign), in Marie-Louise Mallet, ed., *La Démocratie à venir. Autour de Jacques Derrida* (Democracy to Come: Around Jacques Derrida) (Paris: Galilée, 2004), p. 472. My translation. This essay consists of extracts from two sessions of a seminar on "The Beast and the Sovereign" taught by Derrida in Paris during 2001–2.

9   "Autoimmunity: Real and Symbolic Suicides – A Dialogue with Jacques Derrida," in Giovanna Borradori, ed., *Philosophy in a Time of Terror: Dialogues with Jürgen Habermas and Jacques Derrida* (Chicago: University of Chicago Press, 2003), p. 94.

10 "To come to terms with responsibility, then, requires breaking with the horizon of subjectivity, or at least referring the experience of subjectivity – decision, choice, agency – to a constitutive alterity that precedes it and that it cannot comprehend. . . . Others and their traces are always working within us already, in a space and time that cannot be reduced to that of a consciousness or self-presence" – Thomas Keenan, *Fables of Responsibility: Aberrations and Predicaments in Ethics and Politics* (Stanford: Stanford University Press, 1997), p. 66. Keenan's deconstructive discussions of subjectivity and alterity are lucid, although his de Manian attribution of alterity ultimately to language ("rhetoric, text, literature, or fable") is too restrictive. Alterity arrives with time, the other, others, and the unconscious as well as with language in a contretemps. Heteronomy multiply grounds autonomy.

11 On the sovereignty of future cities of refuge and asylum, see Derrida's address to the International Parliament of Writers at Strasbourg in 1996 in his *On Cosmopolitanism and Forgiveness*, trans. Mark Dooley and Michael Hughes (London: Verso, 2001), esp. pp. 4–8. On the necessary sovereignty of the university, see Derrida's "The University without Condition," in *Without Alibi*, esp. pp. 206–7, 232, 235–6.

12 Sovereignty pertains to the domicile: "No hospitality, in the classic sense, without sovereignty of oneself over one's home" – Jacques Derrida, *Of Hospitality: Anne*

Dufourmantelle Invites Jacques Derrida to Respond, trans. Rachel Bowlby (1997; Stanford: Stanford University Press, 2000), p. 55. This book contains two seminar lectures by Derrida from January 1996 accompanied on the facing page with commentary from Dufourmantelle.

13   Rodolphe Gasché, *The Tain of the Mirror: Derrida and the Philosophy of Reflection* (Cambridge: Harvard University Press, 1986), p. 317.

14   In the late works, Derrida often speaks from the perspective of European politics, most prominently in *The Other Heading: Reflections on Today's Europe*, trans. Pascale-Anne Brault and Michael B. Naar (1991; Bloomington: Indiana University Press, 1992), esp. pp. 76–80. This book contains an address of May 1990 to a colloquium on European Cultural Identity, and an interview from January 1989. Derrida remained resolutely and self-consciously Eurocentric in philosophy and politics. For an unsympathetic account of Derrida's politics, particularly dismissive of his messianic view of justice, see Mark Lilla, "The Politics of Jacques Derrida," *New York Review of Books* 45.11, June 25, 1998, which concludes, "Derrida is some vague sort of left democrat who values 'difference' and, as his recent short pamphlet on cosmopolitanism shows, he is committed to seeing Europe become a more open, hospitable place, not least for immigrants. These are not remarkable ideas" (p. 40). Lilla does not mention "sovereignty."

15   Jacques Derrida, *Politics of Friendship*, trans. George Collins (1994; London: Verso, 1997), pp. 304–5. This book grew out of a 1988–9 seminar of the same title, parts of which appeared prior to book publication as addresses and printed articles.

16   A good biographical source is Catherine Malabou and Jacques Derrida, *La Contre-allée* (Counterpath) (Paris: La Quinzaine Littéraire and Louis Vuitton, 1999). This text provides an uncritical overview, yet rich sampler of Derrida's work, with four dozen photos mostly from his personal collection, plus 15 postcards and letters from him during the period 1997–8 to Malabou (a French Hegel scholar), and a concluding curriculum vitae of Derrida.

17   Jacques Derrida, *Specters of Marx: The State of Debt, The Work of Mourning, and the New International*, trans. Peggy Kamuf (1993; New York: Routledge, 1994), p. 84. This book originated as a two-part plenary address to an April 1993 conference on Wither Marxism?

18   According to Derrida, "From that moment, no doubt, dates the feeling, the wish, for solitude, for withdrawal in relation to any community, indeed to any nationality, and the sentiment of suspicion in regard even to this word 'community'" – Jacques Derrida, *Sur parole: Instantanés philosophiques* (On My Word: Philosophical Snapshots) (Paris: L'Aube, 1999, 2005), p. 16. My translation. Compare the "community without unity," framed in the context of social democracy, of William Corlett, *Community without Unity: A Politics of*

Derridean Extravagance (Durham: Duke University Press, 1989), esp. ch. 10. For a concise comparison of Derrida's politics with that of Deleuze and Guattari, see Paul Patton, "Future Politics," in Paul Patton and John Protevi, eds, *Between Deleuze and Derrida* (London: Continuum, 2003), pp. 14–29.

19 Jacques Derrida, "Marx and Sons," in Michael Sprinker, ed., *Ghostly Demarcations: A Symposium on Jacques Derrida's* Specters of Marx (London: Verso, 1999), p. 265 n28. Derrida responds to his nine critics (pp. 213–69, which include 90 notes), complaining at midpoint "I shall have to step up the pace if I am to avoid making a detailed, attentive response filling hundreds of pages (that is, indeed, what is called for, but I have not been allotted the space)" (p. 233).

20 On the vitality for contemporary politics of the new social movements versus party politics, see Immanuel Wallerstein, *Geopolitics and Geoculture: Essays on the Changing World-System* (New York: Cambridge University Press, 1991), pp. 229–30; Ernesto Laclau and Chantal Mouffe, *Hegemony and Socialist Strategy: Towards a Radical Democratic Politics* (London: Verso, 1985), pp. 1–2, 87, 140–1, 159–60; and Michael Hardt and Antonio Negri, *Empire* (Cambridge: Harvard University Press, 2000), p. 272–6.

21 See the analysis and critique of *Specters of Marx* in my *Postmodernism – Local Effects, Global Flows* (Albany: State University of New York Press, 1996), ch. 1. In my *Deconstructive Criticism* (New York: Columbia University Press, 1983), I treat Derrida's early works at length.

Recall that Foucault criticized theories of power based on sovereignty as wrongheaded and blind to modern capillary biopower: "At bottom, despite the differences in epochs and objectives, the representation of power has remained under the spell of monarchy. In political thought and analysis, we still have not cut off the head of the king. Hence the importance that the theory of power gives to the problem of right and violence, law and illegality, freedom and will, and especially the state and sovereignty " – Michel Foucault, *The History of Sexuality, Volume 1: An Introduction*, trans. Robert Hurley (1976; New York: Vintage, 1978), pp. 88–9. A Foucauldian critique of Derridean politics would require a separate study. For a critical overview of Foucault's thinking about sovereignty, see Jean Terrel, "Les figures de la souveraineté," in Guillaume le Blanc and Jean Terrel, eds, *Foucault au Collège de France. Un itinéraire* (Pessac: Presses Universitaires de Bordeaux, 2003), pp. 101–29.

22 The concept of sovereignty quietly presupposes ownership of private property, a feature mentioned unfortunately only in passing by Derrida. See Dan Philpott, "Sovereignty," in Edward N. Zalta, ed., *Stanford Encyclopedia of Philosophy* (Summer 2003 edn), at plato.stanford.edu/archives/ sum/2003/entries/sovereignty. There is a rich history of "sovereignty" as a political concept dating from Machiavelli, Luther, Bodin, and Hobbes up to the present, as Philpott makes clear, although he omits some influential texts, for example, Carl

Schmitt, *Political Theology: Four Chapters on the Concept of Sovereignty*, trans. George Schwab (1922; Cambridge: MIT Press, 1985), and Giorgio Agamben, *Homo Sacer: Sovereign Power and Bare Life*, trans. Daniel Heller-Roazen (1995; Stanford: Stanford University Press, 1998). Schmitt famously opens chapter 1 declaring "Sovereign is he who decides on exception" (p. 5).

23 See, for example, Derrida's "Marx and Sons," pp. 242 and 251; *Without Alibi*, p. 260; and *De quoi demain*, ch. 6 ("L'esprit de la Révolution"), esp. pp. 138–9.

24 Early on I was a follower of Derrida's public intellectual work with both the Group for Research on Philosophic Teaching and the International College of Philosophy in Paris. See my "Deconstruction and Pedagogy," in Cary Nelson, ed., *Theory in the Classroom* (Urbana: University of Illinois Press, 1986), pp. 45–56, and my "Research and Education at the Crossroads: Report on the Collège International de Philosophie," *Substance: A Review of Theory and Literary Criticism* 50 (1986): 101–14.

25 Gayatri Chakravorty Spivak, "Deconstruction and Cultural Studies," in Nicholas Royle, ed., *Deconstructions: A User's Guide* (New York: Palgrave, 2000), p. 35. Spivak melodramatically depicts the end of comparative literature in her Wellek Library Lectures of May 2000 titled *Death of a Discipline* (New York: Columbia University Press, 2003), where she, like Derrida, critically assesses the nation-state (in her case vis-à-vis globalization and the "region" à la Area Studies). Of cultural studies, she complains it is "monolingual, presentist, narcissistic, not practiced enough in close reading even to understand that the mother tongue is actively divided" (p. 20). For Spivak, language, like culture, undetermined and performative, agonistic and heterogeneous, figures collectivity.

26 See, for example, the feminist post-Marxist deconstructions of politics and economics in J. K. Gibson-Graham, *The End of Capitalism (As We Knew It): A Feminist Critique of Political Economy* (Cambridge: Blackwell, 1996), esp. ch. 6, "Querying Globalization," where the two authors set out "to reject globalization as the inevitable inscription of capitalism" (p. 139); and also J.K. Gibson-Graham, Stephen Resnick, and Richard D. Wolff, eds, *Re/Presenting Class: Essays in Postmodern Marxism* (Durham: Duke University Press, 2001), esp. chs 1 and 7: "We would like to deploy our language of class in a project of undermining capitalocentrism and unmaking the global capitalist economy as a discursively hegemonic entity" (p. 170).

During his famous 1983 lecture "The Principle of Reason: The University in the Eyes of Its Pupils," trans. Catherine Porter and Edward P. Morris, available in his collection of diverse pieces on education, *Eyes of the University: Right to Philosophy 2*, trans. Jan Plug et al. (Stanford: Stanford University Press, 2004), Derrida sounds a revealing note of caution at one point: "We are in an implacable political topography: one step further in view of greater profundity or radicalization, even going beyond the 'profound' and the 'radical,' the principial, the *arche*, one step further toward a sort of original an-archy risks producing or reproducing the hierarchy. 'Thinking' requires *both* the principle of reason *and* what is beyond the principle of reason, the *arche* and an-archy" (p. 153).

27 With this roguocracy, "we have here all the ingredients for a counter-concept of sovereignty, à la Bataille" (*Voyous*, p. 100). Bataille's anti-Hegelian project nicknamed "sovereignty," a precursor to deconstruction and more properly named "anti-sovereignty" (subversion and disorder), is examined with admiration by Derrida early on in his "From Restricted to General Economy: A Hegelianism without Reserve," in *Writing and Difference*, trans. Alan Bass (1967; Chicago: University of Chicago Press, 1978), pp. 251–77.

Chapter 6   The Politics of Academic Labor

This chapter started life as an address to a forum on academic labor and theory hosted by the Modern Language Association Committee on the Status of Graduate Students in the Profession. Published in *Critical Inquiry* 31.2 (2005), it has been revised.

1 Here as elsewhere in this book, I am using "disorganization" to describe disaggregation and its mystifications resulting from today's neoclassical/free- market/ neoliberal economic practices. These range from restructuring, deregulation, and outsourcing to privatization, union busting, and temping to 401(k)-style individual "pensions," growing group and salary differentials at workplaces, and rampant sauve-qui-peut free agent codes of professional conduct. Such disorganization characterizes the system of late capitalism, including the higher education sector. See Tom Peters, *Liberation Management: Necessary Disorganization for the Nanosecond Nineties* (New York: Knopf, 1992), esp. part 5, for a representative new management theory rooted in a laissez-faire ideology of disorganization (subcontracting, temporary contracts, fast projects, and quick-changing fashion and opportunism as positive models).

2 Coalition of Graduate Employee Unions, *Casual Nation: A Report*, Dec. 12, 2000, pp. 1–2, at www.cgeu.org.

3 Gary Rhoades, *Managed Professionals: Unionized Faculty and Restructuring Academic Labor* (Albany: State University of New York Press, 1998), pp. 134–6; Gary Rhoades and Sheila Slaughter, "Academic Capitalism, Managed Professionals, and Supply-Side Higher Education," *Social Text* 51 (1997): 20, Special Issue on Academic Labor.

4 Rhoades, *Managed Professionals*, p. 10.

5 Coalition of Graduate Employee Unions, *Casual Nation*, p. 1.

6   John Guillory, "Preprofessionalism: What Graduate Students Want," in *Profession 1996* (New York: Modern Language Association, 1996), pp. 91–9; and MLA Ad Hoc Committee on the Professionalization of PhDs, "Professionalism in Perspective," in *Profession 2000* (New York: Modern Language Association, 2000), pp. 187–210.

7   In Andrew Ross's assessment, "few within academe are in the habit of making links between the corporatization of the modern university and the corresponding shifts in its labor infrastructure. The Yale strikes have changed all that, and now mark a turning point" – "The Labor behind the Cult of Work," *Social Text* 49 (Winter 1996): 25. According to Gordon Lafer's estimate of Yale's academic workforce at the time, "the use of graduate teachers produced savings of over $5 million per year and allowed administrators to eliminate nearly two hundred junior faculty positions at that school alone" – "Graduate Student Unions Fight the Corporate University," *Dissent* 48.4 (Fall 2001): 65.

8   See the Yale Strike Dossier, *Social Text* 49 (1996), 1–131, consisting of ten articles. This special issue was expanded by seven articles and published as Cary Nelson, ed., *Will Teach for Food: Academic Labor in Crisis* (Minneapolis: University of Minnesota Press, 1997). For accounts by strike leaders, see Cynthia Young, "On Strike at Yale," *Minnesota Review* 45–6 (1996): 179–95, and Corey Robin, "Blacklisted and Blue: On Theory and Practice at Yale," in Benjamin Johnson, Patrick Kavanagh, and Kevin Mattson, eds, *Steal This University: The Rise of the Corporate University and the Academic Labor Movement* (New York: Routledge, 2003), pp. 107–22. On the immediate reaction of the Modern Language Association leadership to events surrounding the strike, see Crystal Bartolovich, " 'In This Life We Want Nothing but Facts . . . ' " *Journal X* 2.2 (Spring 1998): 219–35. The apprenticeship model of graduate Teaching Assistantships is widely abused in US universities. It needs to be replaced by an employee model.

9   Vincent B. Leitch et al. (eds), *Norton Anthology of Theory and Criticism* (New York: W.W. Norton, 2001), p. xxxiii. I expand the definition of theory during the course of this chapter as elsewhere in this book.

10 Numerous theories are pertinent here such as Althusser's take on education as the main ideological battleground of contemporary society; Bourdieu's concept of cultural capital as essential to modern class advancement; and Lyotard's trenchant critique of the commercialized university in its current disorganized postmodern condition. See Louis Althusser, "Ideology and Ideological State Apparatuses," in *"Lenin and Philosophy" and Other Essays*, trans. Ben Brewster (New York: Monthly Review, 1971), pp. 127–86; Pierre Bourdieu, *Distinction: A Social Critique of the Judgement of Taste*, trans. Richard Nice (Cambridge: Harvard University Press, 1984); and Jean-François Lyotard, *The Postmodern Condition: A Report on Knowledge*, trans. Geoff Bennington and Brian Massumi

(Minneapolis: University of Minnesota Press, 1984). Earlier figures from Plato to Christine de Pizan to Marx address advanced education in still relevant ways. Figures closer to home like Henry Giroux and bell hooks have published many critiques of contemporary US higher education and labor.

11   MLA Committee on Professional Employment, *Final Report*, Dec. 1997, at www.mla.org. For critiques of this MLA report, see Marc Bousquet et al., "The Institution as False Horizon," *Workplace: A Journal for Academic Labor* 1.1 (Feb. 1998): 6–10, at www.cust.edu.ubc.ca/workplace, and Cary Nelson, "What Hath English Wrought: The Corporate University's Fast Food Discipline," *Workplace: A Journal for Academic Labor* 1.1 (Feb. 1998): 1–24, esp. p. 10: "English more than any other discipline has helped pave the way for the alternative academic workplace and the full proletarianization of the professoriate. About this, the MLA's committee has not a clue."

12   See, for example, *Social Text*'s 1996 Yale Strike Dossier listed in note 8, and the issue on "Activism and the Academy," *Minnesota Review* 50–1 (Oct. 1999).

13   Marc Bousquet, "The Waste Product of Graduate Education: Toward a Dictatorship of the Flexible," *Social Text* 70 (2002): 86. See also Bousquet, "The Rhetoric of 'Job Market' and the Reality of the Academic Labor System," *College English* 66.2 (Nov. 2003): "Under the actually existing system of academic work, the university clearly does not prefer the best or most experienced teachers, it prefers the cheapest teachers" (p. 222). For a forum consisting of a dozen articles centered on four essays by Bousquet, see Special Issue on Information University: Rise of the Education Management Organization, ed. Teresa Derrickson, *Works and Days* 21.1–2 (2003). The Afterword by Bousquet calls for, among other things, a project of "affective mapping" that links TAs' personal feelings of desperation, betrayal, and anxiety to the objective conditions of their work (pp. 361–9).

14   AAUP Committee G, "Report: On the Status of Non-Tenure-Track Faculty," *Academe* 78.6 (1992): 39–48, esp. p. 47. This report does not address TA labor. See, however, AAUP Statement on Graduate Students (2000), which recommends standards on work time, benefits, collective bargaining, governance, etc. This document was widely disseminated, appearing, for example, in *MLA Newsletter* 33.2 (Summer 2001): 4–5. See esp. AAUP Statement on Contingent Appointments and the Academic Profession (2003), at www.aaup.org. See also Cary Nelson, "Lessons from the Job Wars: What Is to Be Done?" *Academe* 81.6 (1995): 18–25.

15   Nelson, "What Hath English Wrought," p. 5: "PhDs are produced in large numbers meanwhile, not because of a massive demand for new faculty but because of an institutional demand for cheap graduate student labor and because of faculty desire to maintain the perks and pleasures of graduate education. It's basically a pyramid scheme." For radical Marxist critiques of

Nelson's labor theory as reformist (not revolutionary) true to its trade unionist roots, see Mas'ud Zavarzadeh, "The Dead Center: *The Chronicle of Higher Education* and the 'Radical' in the Academy," *The Alternative Orange* 5.2 (Summer/Fall 1997), Special Issue on the Privatization of Public Education: Capitalism and Its Knowledge and Industries, at www.geocities.com/redtheory/AO/AOVol5-2.html; and Brian Ganter, "Haven't You Realized That Workers Have It Pretty Good Today?" *Red Critique* 1 (Spring 2001): 29–33.

16 On the situation of labor, see André Gorz's prophetic *Farewell to the Working Class*, trans. Michael Sonenscher (1980; Boston: South End, 1982): "A society based on mass unemployment is coming into being before our eyes. It consists of a growing mass of the permanently unemployed on one hand, an aristocracy of tenured workers on the other, and, between them, a proletariat of temporary workers carrying out the least skilled and most unpleasant types of work" (p. 3). See also Jeremy Rifkin's more recent *The End of Work: The Decline of the Global Labor Force and the Dawn of the Post-Market Era* (New York: Putnam's, 1995), esp. part 4. See, however, Jacques Derrida, "The University without Condition," in *Without Alibi*, ed. and trans. Peggy Kamuf (Stanford: Stanford University Press, 2002): "Rifkin does not speak of unemployed teachers or aspiring professors, in particular in the Humanities. He pays no attention to the growing marginalization of so many part-time employees, all underpaid and marginalized in the university, in the name of what is called flexibility or competitivity" (p. 226). See also Ulrich Beck, *The Brave New World of Work*, trans. Patrick Camiller (Cambridge: Polity, 2000): "Calls are made everywhere for greater 'flexibility' – or, in other words, that employers should be able to fire employees with less difficulty. Flexibility also means a redistribution of risks away from the state and the economy towards the individual. The jobs on offer become short-term and easily terminable (i.e. 'renewable')" (p. 3). See also David Harvey, *A Brief History of Neoliberalism* (New York: Oxford University Press, 2005): "Under neoliberalization, the figure of the 'disposable worker' emerges as prototypical upon the world stage" (p. 169).

17 Vincent B. Leitch, "The PhD and Jobs," *MLA Newsletter* 4 (Sept. 1972): 7–8.

18 It was less clear during the 1970s than now that academic administrators would "produce a system that – while financially successful – has undercut much of what used to stand at the heart of academic life" (Lafer, "Graduate Student Unions Fight the Corporate University," p. 65). In "The Drain-O of Higher Education: Casual Labor and University Teaching," Benjamin Johnson also points his finger at academic administrators: "So the employment crisis – most of it, perhaps all of it – is not the product of the iron hand of supply and demand, but rather the result of universities' decisions to slough off work that should be done by regular faculty onto adjuncts, postdocs, and graduate students" (Johnson, Kavanagh, and Mattson, *Steal This University*, p. 67).

19 See, for example, the panicked report from the 1970 MLA Commission to Study the Job Market authored by David Orr, "The Job Market in English and Foreign Languages," *PMLA* 85 (1970): 1185–98.

20 See William G. Bowen and Julie Ann Sosa, *Prospects for Faculty in the Arts and Sciences: A Study of Factors Affecting Demand and Supply, 1987–2012* (Princeton: Princeton University Press, 1989), a widely influential optimistic prediction, which Bousquet criticizes in detail ("The Rhetoric of 'Job Market'").

21 "Under Clinton's presidency, the decline in the number of people receiving food stamps – 9.8 million – was 17 percent greater than the decline in the number of people officially defined as impoverished, and was accompanied by a dramatic increase in the pressure on private soup kitchens and food pantries" – Robert Pollin, *Contours of Descent: US Economic Fractures and the Landscape of Global Austerity* (New York: Verso, 2003), p. 30.

22 See, to cite only a few well-known examples, Stuart Hall and Martin Jacques, eds, *New Times: The Changing Face of Politics in the 1990s* (London: Verso, 1990); David Harvey, "The Political-Economic Transformation of Late Twentieth-Century Capitalism," in *The Condition of Postmodernity* (Cambridge: Blackwell, 1990), pp. 19–97; Immanuel Wallerstein, *Geopolitics and Geoculture: Essays on the Changing World-System* (New York: Cambridge University Press, 1991); Fredric Jameson, *Postmodernism, or, the Cultural Logic of Late Capitalism* (Durham: Duke University Press, 1991); Arjun Appadurai, *Modernity at Large: Cultural Dimensions of Globalization* (Minneapolis: University of Minnesota Press, 1996); Pierre Bourdieu, *Acts of Resistance: Against the Tyranny of the Market*, trans. Richard Nice (New York: New Press, 1999); and Michael Hardt and Antonio Negri, *Empire* (Cambridge: Harvard University Press, 2000). My own work in this area includes "Transformations in Political Economy during Postmodern Times," in *Postmodernism – Local Effects, Global Flows* (Albany: State University of New York Press, 1996), pp. 145–57, and "The New Economic Criticisms," in *Theory Matters* (New York: Routledge, 2003), pp. 107–22.

According to Lisa Featherstone and Doug Henwood: "As a field, economics has become increasingly hostile to unorthodox opinion in recent years, and virtually no left of center economist has been hired by a major [US] department in more than two decades" – "Clothes Encounter: Activists and Economists Clash over Sweatshops," *Lingua Franca: The Review of Academic Life* 11 (Mar. 2001): 31. Regarding sweatshops, the campaign on behalf of fair wages for garment workers needs to be extended to casual and service workers.

23 For critiques of the unelected IMF, see among many others the economists Robin Hahnel, *Panic Rules! Everything You Need to Know about the Global Economy* (Cambridge: South End, 1999), ch. 6, and Nobel Prize winner Joseph E. Stiglitz, *Globalization and Its Discontents* (New York: W. W. Norton, 2002).

24   In the face of such changes, there have been increasing calls for cultural studies scholars and public intellectuals to intervene in policy decision-making. See, for example, Michael Bérubé, *The Employment of English: Theory, Jobs, and the Future of Literary Studies* (New York: New York University Press, 1998): "This then has been my fixation since the elections of 1994: configuring the relations among American cultural studies, the latest policy initiatives of the New Right, and the discourse of the public intellectual. I want to argue that cultural studies, if it is going to be anything more than just one more intellectual paradigm for the reading of literary and cultural texts, must direct its attention to the local and national machinery of public policy" (p. 224). See also Masao Miyoshi, "Ivory Tower in Escrow," *boundary 2* 27.1 (2000): 7–50, for a critique of the silence of theory and the humanities regarding the degraded conditions of academic labor and the corporatization of the university. In "What It Is and What It Isn't: Cultural Studies Meets Graduate-Student Labor," *Yale Journal of Law & Humanities* 13.1 (2001): 69–94, Toby Miller refutes criticisms of cultural studies for its being irrelevant and nonpolitical. He cites its role in graduate student unionizing at New York University (his home institution) during the landmark four-year campaign from 1998 to 2002. On this campaign, see Lisa Jessup, "The Campaign for Union Rights at NYU," in Johnson, Kavanagh, and Mattson, *Steal This University*, pp. 145–70. For a discussion of campus labor activist groups and movements, such as Coalition on Contingent Academic Labor, California Part-Time Faculty Association, Coalition on the Academic Workforce, and Campus Equity Week, see Eileen E. Schell, "Every Week Should Be Campus Equity Week: Toward a Labor Theory of Agency in Higher Education," *Works and Days* 21.1–2 (2003): 313–37.

     On the relations between theory and academic working conditions, Michael Bérubé in *Rhetorical Occasions: Essays on Humans and the Humanities* (Chapel Hill: University of North Carolina Press, 2006) declares "the fact that other scholars work in queer theory or pledge allegiance to Deleuze and Agamben does not harm me, or literature, in the slightest. I care far more about disparities in the basic working conditions of my fellow scholars . . . than about intellectual disparities between scholars who develop an epistemology of the closet and scholars who study medieval lives of the saints" (p. 151).

25   During the course of the 1990s, points out Andrew Ross, "the concept of a finite workday had been obliterated by 24/7 access to networks of information. Even worse, time poverty was becoming a mark of stature. Whereas persons of leisure had once enjoyed the highest social status, now it was prestigious to be too busy" – *No-Collar: The Humane Workplace and Its Hidden Costs* (New York: Basic Books, 2003), p. 44.

26   Stanley Aronowitz, "The Last Good Job in America," in Randy Martin, ed., *Chalk Lines: The Politics of Work in the Managed University* (Durham: Duke University Press, 1998), p. 216.
27   Scrap tenure. The widespread reliance on casual labor erodes tenure. Moreover, many beginning North American academics now regard tenure as a class barrier not worth defending. Thus the long-term well-being and future of academic tenure appear in doubt. "Ultimately, the comfort offered by job security in the form of tenure was a recipe for complacency on the part of those who might have resisted the casualization measures, much earlier and more vigorously. Submission to the selfless, disinterested devotions of the scholar's calling almost inevitably led to the sacrifice of younger 'apprentices' on the altar of an anachronistic faith" – Andrew Ross, *Low Pay, High Profile: The Global Push for Fair Labor* (New York: New Press, 2004), pp. 222–3.
28   Few academics seem aware of the disorganization and privatization during recent years of the leading US higher education retirement fund, the 3.5 million-participant TIAA–CREF (Teachers Insurance and Annuity Association–College Retirement and Equities Fund), whose latest CEO received in excess of 4 million dollars in wages for his first year, 2003, a year noteworthy for 500 layoffs (8% of the company's workforce).

Chapter 7   Late Contemporary US Poetry

1   Among the attacks on the Iowa Writer's Workshop poem, one of the most notable is from Donald Hall, "Poetry and Ambition," *Kenyon Review* 5 (1983), reprinted in his *Poetry and Ambition: Essays 1982–1988*, Poets on Poetry series (Ann Arbor: University of Michigan Press, 1988), pp. 1–19. Hall famously coins the sarcastic term "Mc Poem" and calls for the destruction of Iowa and the M.F.A. in creative writing.
2   Mark Wallace, "Toward a Free Multiplicity of Form," in M. Wallace and Steven Marks, eds, *Telling It Slant: Avant-Garde Poetics of the 1990s*, Modern and Contemporary Poetics series (Tuscaloosa: University of Alabama Press, 2002), p. 193.
3   See, for example, Fredric Jameson, *Postmodernism, or, the Cultural Logic of Late Capitalism* (Durham: Duke University Press, 1991); David Harvey, *The Condition of Postmodernity* (Cambridge: Blackwell, 1990); and my *Postmodernism – Local Effects, Global Flows* (Albany: State University of New York Press, 1996). See also Stephen Burt, "American Writing Today: Poetry," *n+1* 4 (Spring 2006): 71–5, which argues for dividing contemporary US poetry into two distinct periods, 1945–72 and 1973–present: " 'Today' begins around 1973" (p. 74).

4   Dana Gioia, David Mason, and Meg Schoerke, eds, *Twentieth-Century American Poetry* (Boston: McGraw-Hill, 2004), p. 664. See also the substantial companion volume compiled by Gioia, Mason, and Schoerke, eds, *Twentieth-Century American Poetics: Poets on the Art of Poetry* (Boston: McGraw-Hill, 2004).

5   Paul Lauter, gen. ed., *The Heath Anthology of American Literature*, 5th edn, vol. E (Contemporary Period: 1945 to the Present) (Boston: Houghton Mifflin, 2006), p. 1886.

6   Jahan Ramazani, Richard Ellmann, and Robert O'Clair, eds, *Norton Anthology of Modern and Contemporary Poetry*, 3rd edn, vol. 2 (New York: W. W. Norton, 2003), p. xliii. In *Postmodern American Poetry: A Norton Anthology* (New York: W. W. Norton, 1994), editor Paul Hoover defines "postmodernism" not as a period, the way I do following Jameson and others, but as a particular style or aesthetic mode synonymous with late twentieth-century neo-avant-gardes and with experimentalism. "Postmodernist poetry is the avant-garde of our time" (p. xxv); it "opposes the centrist values of unity, significance, linearity, expressiveness, and a heightened, even heroic, portrayal of the bourgeois self and its concerns" (p. xxvii). When comparing the above two anthologies, Alan Golding, in *From Outlaw to Classic: Canons in American Poetry* (Madison: University of Wisconsin Press, 1995), underscores the present-day "tendency of editors and publishers to map the poetic landscape by reference to parallel but separate rivers," and thus highlights "the pluralism that has created the impossibility of broadly inclusive or representative collections" (p. 35).

7   See Jack W. C. Hagstrom and Bill Morgan, eds, *Dana Gioia: A Descriptive Bibliography with Critical Essays* (Jackson: Parrish House, 2002); April Lindner, *Dana Gioia*, Western Writers series, no. 143 (Boise: Boise State University, 2000). The Hagstrom–Morgan detailed bibliography offers also four critical essays, including poet-philosopher H. L. Hix's "Dana Gioia's Criticism," a cogent overview that concludes "Dana Gioia has produced – and is producing – a body of criticism as important and influential as that of any living poet-critic" (p. 296).

8   Dana Gioia, "Business and Poetry," in *Can Poetry Matter? Essays on Poetry and American Culture*, Tenth Anniversary Edition (1992; St Paul: Graywolf Press, 2002), pp. 101–24. Hereafter *CPM*.

9   Dana Gioia, "Disappearing Ink: Poetry at the End of Print Culture," in *Disappearing Ink: Poetry at the End of Print Culture* (St Paul: Graywolf Press, 2004), p. 7. Hereafter *DI*.

10   Charles Bernstein, "The Academy in Peril: William Carlos Williams Meets the MLA," in *Contents Dream: Essays 1975–1984* (Los Angeles: Sun & Moon Press, 1986), pp. 244–51. Against mainstream poetry, Bernstein, a spokesperson for Language poetry, here calls for heteroglot discourses, loosened genre codes, and ruptured syntax cut free from the conventional isolated lyric voice expressing personal feeling. A businessman-poet for nearly two decades like

Gioia, Bernstein is also critical of the established institutions of poetry (publishers, review outlets, writing programs, prize committees), in the name, however, not of popular poetry but of language-centered vanguardism stemming from the lines of Williams-Stein-Zukofsky-Spicer plus poststructuralism. In our era of zapping, the creation of linguistic collages resembles the discontinuous catalogues of the standup comedian. It is a matter of disconnected bits, fast-moving parataxes, the dominant trope of Language poetry.

11   Vincent B. Leitch, "Blues Southwestern Style," in *Theory Matters* (New York: Routledge, 2003), pp. 137–64. See also Kevin Young, ed., *Blues Poems* (New York: Knopf, 2003).

12   For a wide-ranging account of fin-de-siècle experimental vanguard poetries, see both volumes by Hank Lazer, *Opposing Poetries*, vol. 1: *Issues and Institutions*; vol. 2: *Readings*, Avant-Garde and Modernism Studies series (Evanston: Northwestern University Press, 1996). Opposing poetries, by definition, "critique and contest assumptions and practices of more mainstream poetries" (vol. 1, p. 1). They include here feminist poetries, Language poetry, and ethnopoetics, plus oral and performance poetries. Beyond Gioia's populist poetries, they resist not only official verse culture, but also "the marketplace, the dominant culture, and hegemonic ideologies" (vol. 1, p. 56).

   Counted among contemporary US experimentalist and vanguardist poets also should be second- and third-generation writers of earlier schools like Beat, Black Mountain, and New York poetry; aleatory, procedural, and visual poetry; and digital poetries (hypertext, visual-kinetic text, programmable works). On this latter topic, see Loss Pequeño Glazier, *Digital Poetics: The Making of E-Poetries*, Modern and Contemporary Poetics series (Tuscaloosa: University of Alabama Press, 2002): "The term 'poetry' is used in this volume to refer to practices of innovative poetry rather than to what might be called academic, formal, or traditional forms of poetry" (p. 181 n1). See also Adalaide Morris and Thomas Swiss, eds, *New Media Poetics: Contexts, Technotexts, and Theories* (Cambridge: MIT Press, 2006).

13   Dana Gioia, *Barrier of a Common Language: An American Looks at Contemporary British Poetry*, Poets on Poetry series (Ann Arbor: University of Michigan Press, 2003), p. 82.

14   Marjorie Perloff, *21st-Century Modernism: The "New" Poetics* (Malden: Blackwell, 2002), p. 161. Perloff continues with a succinct characterization of the style of today's dominant verse culture: "The language is usually concrete and colloquial, the ironies and metaphors multiple, the syntax straightforward, the rhythms muted and low-key. Generic and media boundaries are rigorously observed" (pp. 161–2). A defender of experimental modernism and associated interarts poetry, Perloff characterizes such contemporary workshop poetry as approaching journalism (p. 164).

15 Theodor W. Adorno, "On Lyric Poetry and Society" (1957), in *Notes to Literature*, vol. 1, ed. Rolf Tiedemann, trans. Shierry Weber Nicholsen (1958, rev. edn 1968; New York: Columbia University Press, 1991), p. 45.

16 Walter Kalaidjian, *Languages of Liberation: The Social Text in Contemporary American Poetry* (New York: Columbia University Press, 1989), p. 32. See also Walter Kalaidjian, *American Culture between the Wars: Revisionary Modernism and Postmodern Critique* (New York: Columbia University Press, 1993), esp. ch. 4, "Transpersonal Poetics."

17 Jed Rasula, *Syncopations: The Stress of Innovation in Contemporary American Poetry*, Modern and Contemporary Poetics series (Tuscaloosa: University of Alabama Press, 2004), p. 24. In his earlier wide-ranging history, *The American Poetry Wax Museum: Reality Effects, 1940–1990* (Urbana: National Council of Teachers of English, 1996), Rasula observed: "In the neopuritan atmosphere of postwar American poetry the capitalization of the speaking subject becomes an obsessional neurosis, a hankering for a capitol to serve as F.D.I.C. of cultural capital. It is also the great preoccupation of anthologists, as they continue to deny, in every way they can, the advent of the decentered subject" (p. 37).

18 Michael Davidson, *Ghostlier Demarcations: Modern Poetry and the Material Word* (Berkeley: University of California Press, 1997), p. 227. In a nod to Michel Foucault, Davidson defines "technologies of presence" as "those systems of production and reproduction within which the voice achieves enough autonomy to regard itself as present–unto–itself" (p. 199).

19 Charles Altieri, *Postmodernisms Now: Essays on Contemporaneity in the Arts* (University Park: Pennsylvania State University Press, 1998), p. 11. See also Charles Altieri, *The Art of Twentieth-Century American Poetry: Modernism and After* (Malden: Blackwell, 2006). The latter book examines the many facets of poetic subjectivity up to 1980 on the premise that the self is not only socio-historically conditioned and in continuous process, but also psychologically shaped by the imaginary, including the constitutive forces of desire, fantasy, and imagination. Self-knowledge involves projection; self-mastery is a pose. Altieri charts the twists and turns of poetic self and sensibility. According to Stephen Burt, a hallmark phenomenon of US poetry in recent decades is innumerable "poems about the pathos of uncertain epistemology – about not being able to know and recognize a stable, unique, or axiomatic self" – Panel on Poetry Criticism: What Is It For, Poetry Society of America, Mar. 15, 2000, New York City, at www.poetrysociety.org/journal/offpage/vendler-perloff.html.

20 Christopher Beach, *Poetic Culture: Contemporary American Poetry between Community and Institution*, Avant-Garde and Modernism Studies series (Evanston: Northwestern University Press, 1999), p. 132.

21 In his lectures published as *Democracy, Culture and the Voice of Poetry* (Princeton: Princeton University Press, 2002), Robert Pinsky, former US Poet Laureate

and impresario of the populist and wildly popular Favorite Poem Project, attempts to have it both ways. "Poetry, then, has roots in the moment when a voice makes us alert to the presence of another or others. It has affinities with all the ways a solitary voice, actual or virtual, imitates the presence of others. Yet as a form of art it is deeply embedded in the single human voice, in the solitary state that hears the other and sometimes recreates that other. Poetry is a vocal imagining, ultimately social but essentially individual and inward" (p. 39). For Pinsky, moreover, the place of poetry in American culture, having no hereditary aristocracy and no single folk culture but an increasingly broad heterogeneous mass culture, remains unsettled today as it was yesterday.

Chapter 8   Globalization of Literatures

1   On the literary and critical theories of African, Native, Chicano/a, and Asian Americans, including feminist research and scholarship, see the annotated selected bibliographies in Vincent B. Leitch et al. (eds), *Norton Anthology of Theory and Criticism* (New York: W. W. Norton, 2001), pp. 2532ff.

2   Marc Shell and Werner Sollors, eds, *The Multilingual Anthology of American Literature: A Reader of Original Texts with English Translations* (New York: New York University Press, 2000). See Evelyn Nien-Ming Ch'ien, *Weird English* (Cambridge: Harvard University Press, 2004), which examines bi- and poly-lingual contemporary fiction in new forms of English.

3   On slash fiction by working-class and subprofessional women fans of, for example, *Star Trek*, see the landmark study by Constance Penley, "Feminism, Psychoanalysis, and the Study of Popular Culture," in Lawrence Grossberg, Cary Nelson, and Paula Treichler, eds, *Cultural Studies* (New York: Routledge, 1992), pp. 479–94.

4   Paul Gilroy, *The Black Atlantic: Modernity and Double Consciousness* (Cambridge: Harvard University Press, 1993).

5   See, for example, John Carlos Rowe, "Postcolonialism, Globalism, and the New American Studies," in Donald E. Pease and Robyn Wiegman, eds, *The Futures of American Studies* (Durham: Duke University Press, 2002), pp.167–82.

6   Rob Wilson, *Reimagining the American Pacific* (Durham: Duke University Press, 2000).

7   Paul Lauter, gen. ed., *The Heath Anthology of American Literature*, 2nd edn, vols 1 and 2, ed. Richard Yarborough et al. (Lexington: D. C. Heath, 1994).

8   See, for example, the often-cited cultural studies work of both Janice Radway, *Reading the Romance: Women, Patriarchy, and Popular Literature* (1984; Chapel Hill: University of North Carolina Press, 1991), and Andrew Ross, *Strange Weather: Culture, Science, and Technology in the Age of Limits* (New York: Verso, 1991).

The status of new forms of interactive literature, namely hyperfiction, MUDs, MOOs, and role-playing video games, remains uncertain. See, among many sources, the documented skeptical account of Michael Chaouli, "How Interactive Can Fiction Be?" *Critical Inquiry* 31.3 (Spring 2005): 599–617.

9 For the definitive work on the foundations of taste in social class, see Pierre Bourdieu, *Distinction: A Social Critique of the Judgement of Taste*, trans. Richard Nice (Cambridge: Harvard University Press, 1984): "To the socially recognized hierarchy of the arts, and within each of them, of genres, schools or periods, corresponds a social hierarchy of the consumers" (p. 1).

10 On the changing criteria of literary merit during the late twentieth century in the US, see my *Theory Matters* (New York: Routledge, 2003), ch. 1, as well as my background history *American Literary Criticism from the 1930s to the 1980s* (New York: Columbia University Press, 1988).

11 For a critical history of American literature scholarship, see Peter Carafiol, *The American Ideal: Literary History as Worldly Activity* (New York: Oxford University Press, 1991), esp. pp. 42–3 on Americanist scholarship as a nationalistic project.

12 Raymond Williams, "Literature," in *Keywords: A Vocabulary of Culture and Society*, rev. edn (New York: Oxford University Press, 1983), pp. 183–8.

13 An online Google Search of "Black British Literature" turned up 2 million items on February 21, 2007. As an introduction, see the collection of scholarly articles in R. Victoria Arana and Lauri Ramey, eds, *Black British Writing* (New York: Palgrave Macmillan, 2004), esp. chs 2 and 11.

14 As the examples of Joyce and Kafka suggest, minority writers using major languages can act like "free agents" capable of expanding, subverting, and transforming dominant languages, traditions, genres. This is the famous libertarian argument of Gilles Deleuze and Félix Guattari, *Kafka: Toward a Minor Literature*, trans. Dana Polan (Minneapolis: University of Minnesota Press, 1986), ch. 3.

15 On global–local dynamics, see, for instance, Arif Dirlik, "Place-Based Imagination: Globalism and the Politics of Place," *Review* 22.2 (1999): 151–87; and Rob Wilson's *Reimagining the American Pacific*, esp. ch. 4, where he observes "Any version of the *local* or *regional*, as I have been urging in this study, will thus have to be spread on some cognitive map of *global postmodernity*" (p. 137).

16 John Thieme, ed., *The Arnold Anthology of Post-colonial Literatures in English* (London: Arnold, 1996), p. 3. "English literature is now as much a global as a national phenomenon..." notes David Damrosch, *What Is World Literature?* (Princeton: Princeton University Press, 2003), p. 230.

17 See, for example, Scott McCracken, *Pulp: Reading Popular Fiction* (Manchester: Manchester University Press, 1998), which examines detective fiction, romance, science fiction, and horror.

18 Postmodernization and globalization have thrown comparative literature, a metadiscipline dependent on national literatures and languages, into disarray,

as is reflected in much recent scholarship, notably the collective state of the discipline reports from the American Comparative Literature Association – Charles Bernheimer, ed., *Comparative Literature in the Age of Multiculturalism* (Baltimore: Johns Hopkins University Press, 1995), and Haun Saussy, ed., *Comparative Literature in an Age of Globalization* (Baltimore: Johns Hopkins University Press, 2006). See also Gayatri Chakravorty Spivak, *Death of a Discipline* (New York: Columbia University Press, 2003), where Spivak, a comparativist, issues the following wakeup call: "I hope the book will be read as the last gasp of a dying discipline" (p. xii).

On a related topic, much scholarly writing has worried anew the conception of world literature, usually from a metropolitan globalized subject position. See, for example, David Damrosch's *What Is World Literature?*; Pascale Casanova, *The World Republic of Letters*, trans. M. B. DeBevoise (1999; Cambridge: Harvard University Press, 2004); and Christopher Prendergast, ed., *Debating World Literature* (London: Verso, 2004), which contains 15 pieces, including Franco Moretti's galvanizing "Conjectures on World Literature" (2000) that observes "the study of world literature is – inevitably – a study of the struggle for symbolic hegemony across the world" (p. 158).

19 For a much-cited analysis that addresses the role of the canon in social and linguistic stratification and exclusion, and that strenuously deemphasizes its contents, whether liberally expanded or long and conservatively established, see John Guillory, *Cultural Capital: The Problem of Literary Canon Formation* (Chicago: University of Chicago Press, 1993), esp. ch. 1.

20 For two classic descriptions and critiques of postmodern culture, see Fredric Jameson, *Postmodernism, or, the Cultural Logic of Late Capitalism* (Durham: Duke University Press, 1991), and David Harvey, *The Condition of Postmodernity* (Cambridge: Blackwell, 1990).

21 For my account, see Vincent B. Leitch, *Postmodernism – Local Effects, Global Flows* (Albany: State University of New York Press, 1996), and *Theory Matters*, esp. Preface (pp. vii–xi).

22 Roland Robertson traces five phases of globalization from 1400 to the present in *Globalization: Social Theory and Global Culture* (London: Sage, 1992). I discuss the recent literature on globalization in *Theory Matters*, chs 8 and 9.

23 Unlike hyperglobalizers and reformers, skeptics of globalization question the motives and interests driving the very narrative of globalization. See, for example, Paul Hirst and Grahame Thompson, *Globalization in Question* (Cambridge: Polity, 1996), and J. K. Gibson-Graham, *The End of Capitalism (As We Knew It)* (Cambridge: Blackwell, 1996), esp. ch. 6, where the argument seeks "to reject globalization as the inevitable inscription of capitalism" (p. 139).

24 See "Globalizing Literary Studies," special issue of *PMLA* 116.1 (2001), consisting of 12 essays.

25 Arjun Appadurai, *Modernity at Large: Cultural Dimensions of Globalization* (Minneapolis: University of Minnesota Press, 1996), which argues against the thesis that globalization equals (American) homogenization.

26 See Gregory S. Jay, "The Discipline of the Syllabus," in *American Literature and the Culture Wars* (Ithaca: Cornell University Press, 1997), pp. 136–68.

27 See Lisa Lowe, *Immigrant Acts: On Asian American Cultural Politics* (Durham: Duke University Press, 1996), esp. ch. 4. Lowe roundly criticizes official US liberal pluralist multiculturalism for its depoliticizing, dehistoricizing, and homogenizing myth of inclusion; for its deafness to oppositional narratives that stress inequalities among and within different social and ethnic minority groups; and for its premature reconciliation of conflict, dissent, otherness. Also Lowe questions the very notion of "Asian American" while still thematizing "Asian American cultural productions as countersites to US national memory and national culture" (p. 4).

For an overview and bibliographical survey, see the entry "Multiculturalism," in Michael Groden, Martin Kreiswirth, and Imre Szeman, eds, *Johns Hopkins Guide to Literary Theory and Criticism*, 2nd edn (Baltimore: Johns Hopkins University Press, 2005), pp. 666–73. For a sociological case study of four English departments' diverse handling of multiculturalism during the 1990s, see Bethany Bryson, *Making Multiculturalism: Boundaries and Meaning in US English Departments* (Stanford: Stanford University Press, 2005).

Index

cultural studies (*cont'd*)
  and popular culture 116–17
  postmodern 56
  relationship with literary
    and critical theory 23–6,
    50, 61
  and sociology 84
  the spread of 57
  subfields 4, 25, 32
  UK compared with US 23–4
cultural theory
  renaissance of 1
  task of 3, 19–20
  teaching 16–31
culture wars (1980s) 2, 16–17, 57,
  66, 83, 106
curriculum
  informal 18
  theory in the 18–19, 49
cyborg 4, 121, 135

Davidson, Michael 121, 161n
de Certeau, Michel 27
de Man, Paul 11, 66, 83
death penalty 70, 77
debt 79, 93
decolonization 130, 136, 137
deconstruction 2, 10, 11, 68
  in cultural studies 83–4
  Derridean vs. structuralism 65
  of grand narratives 135
  of norms 89
  of the self 120–3
  of sovereignty 69–76
deindustrialization 93
Deleuze, Gilles 10, 26, 27
democracy, and sovereignty 70–6

democracy to come (Derrida) 65,
  69, 74–6, 80–1, 82
democratic socialism 77
departmentalization,
  traditional 58–9, 125
deregulation 79, 93
Derrida, Jacques 4, 10, 26, 27
  De quoi demain... dialogue with
    Roudinesco 67, 73, 74, 76, 81
  deconstruction of sovereignty
    2, 71–6
  evaluation of 80, 81–4
  Genèses, genealogies, genres et le
    génie 67
  interviews and dialogues 67–8
  key concepts 65, 69, 80
  late 65–84
  Negotiations 68, 78, 81
  On Cosmopolitanism and
    Forgiveness 68, 75–6
  Philosophy in a Time of Terror
    71–2, 73, 74, 81–2
  politics 77–81
  Politics of Friendship 68, 76,
    77–8
  Specters of Marx 78–80, 82, 83
  Voyous 67, 69, 71, 72, 73, 81
detective stories 124
dialects 124, 129, 130, 134
diaries 124, 129
différance 65
difference 58, 135, 137
digital poetics 103, 116
disability studies 9, 32
disaggregation 11, 14, 29, 122, 135
  in American poetry 105–20
  of applied theory 33, 36